So

"Though nothing indicates the time of Cecco Angiolieri's death, I will venture to surmise that he outlived the writing and revision of Dante's *Inferno* – if only by the token that he is not found lodged in one of its meaner cricles."
Dante Gabriel Rossetti

"The originality of Cecco lies above all in having made poetry out of his own very special experiences, his most intimate sentiments, with a sincerity that is aggressive and offensive. It is an originality for which good reputation pays a high price. This calls for a sad kind of courage. And Cecco has it, and uses it with a repulsive calm… Angiolieri, for his originality and craftmanship, really deserves to be widely studied."
Luigi Pirandello

"Cecco Angiolieri. Siena. A choleric and blasphemous Tuscan. Fined and taken to law, wasted his paternal inheritance, died in misery. While the poetry of his age celebrated the angelic woman, he praised a tanner's rough daughter. Cultivated insult and abuse; sang of gambling, wine and money, of his hatred for his father and of his curse upon the world."
Antonio Tabucchi

ONEWORLD CLASSICS

Sonnets

Cecco Angiolieri

Translated by

C.H. Scott and Anthony Mortimer

ONEWORLD
CLASSICS

ONEWORLD CLASSICS LTD
London House
243-253 Lower Mortlake Road
Richmond
Surrey TW9 2LL
United Kingdom
www.oneworldclassics.com

This edition first published by Oneworld Classics Limited in 2008
All rights reserved.
Background material and revised translation © Anthony Mortimer, 2008
Translation of excerpt from Boccaccio's *Decameron* © J.G. Nichols, 2008

Printed in Jordan by National Press

ISBN: 978-1-84749-043-8

Contents

Sonnets   1

  Sonnets Ascribed to Cecco Angiolieri   221

  Note on the Text   264

  Notes   266

Extra Material   269

  Cecco Angiolieri's Life   271

  Cecco Angiolieri's Sonnets   273

  Select English Bibliography   278

  Select Italian Bibliography   279

Appendices   281

  Dante Gabriel Rossetti's Translations   283
  of Cecco Angiolieri

  From Boccaccio's Decameron (IX, 4)   297

  Biographical Note on C.H. Scott   301

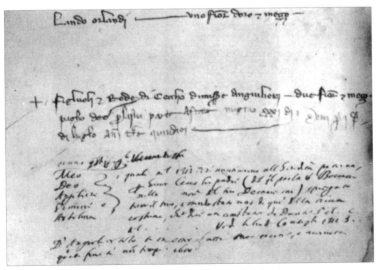

A fifteenth-century manuscript of Cecco Angiolieri's
sonnet 'S'i' fosse foco'

The formal renunciation of Cecco's inheritance
by his children

Sonnets

I

"Accorri accorri accorri, uom, a la strada!"
"Che ha', fi' de la putta?" – "I' son rubato."
"Chi t'ha rubato?" – "Una che par che rada
come rasoio, si m'ha netto lasciato."
"Or come non le davi de la spada?"
"I' dare' anz'a me." – "Or se' 'mpazzato?"
"Non so che 'l dà, così mi par che vada."
"Or t'avess'ella cieco, sciagurato!"
"E vedi che ne pare a que' che 'l sanno?"
"Di' quel che tu mi rubi." – "Or va' con Dio,
ma anda pian, ch'i' vo' pianger lo danno,
ché ti diparti." – "Con animo rio!"
"Tu abbi 'l danno con tutto 'l malanno!"
"Or chi m'ha morto?" – "E che diavol sacc'io?"

I

"Help, help! For God's sake, help! Hi, here in the street!"
"What's up, you whoreson?" – "I've been robbed, I swear."
"Who's robbed you then?" – "A wench who does it neat,
And cleaner than a razor shaves your hair."
"But where's your sword? To kill her would be sweet."
"I'd rather kill myself." – "You're mad, then." – "Yea,
I'm mad, but don't know why" – "So, I repeat,
That wretched girl would take your sight away!"
"A madman, yes, we see you know that part!"
"What have you plundered from me?" – "Go in peace,
But slowly, give me time to mourn this woe
And see you leaving." – "With a bitter heart!"
"Now may your loss with every curse increase!"
"Who killed me?" – "How the devil should I know?"*

II

Or non è gran pistolenza la mia,
ch'i' non mi posso partir dad amare
quella che m'odia e nïente degnare
vuol pur vedere ond'i' passo la via?
E dammi tanta pena, notte e dia,
che de l'angoscia mi fa sì sudare,
che m'arde l'anima, e niente non pare;
certo non credo ch'altro 'nferno sia.
Assa' potrebb'uom dirm': "A nulla giova!"
Ch'ell'è di tale schiatta nata, 'ntendo,
che tutte son di così mala pruova.
Ma per ch'i' la trasamo, pur attendo
ch'Amor alcuna cosa la rimova:
ch'è sì possente che 'l può far correndo.

II

Now is not mine a sorry plight, I say,
Because I've lost the power to refrain
From loving one whose hatred will not deign
To see me when I pass upon my way?
She brings me such great torment night and day
That many a time I even sweat with pain,
My heart is set on fire, and all in vain:
Hell can't be worse, I fancy, come what may.
In truth, it might be said that I'm ill-fated.
Surely she comes of an accursèd breed,
Whose daughters all are pitiless and cunning.
Alas, by now, I'm so infatuated,
I think that Love will change her, for indeed,
He's surely strong enough to do it running.

III

I' ho sì poco di grazia 'n Becchina,
in fé di Di', ch'anche non tèn a frodo,
che in le' non posso trovar via né modo,
né medico mi val né medicina;
ch'ella m'è peggio ch'una saracina
o che non fu a' pargoli il re Rodo;
ma certo tanto di le' me ne lodo,
ch'esser con meco non vorrìe reina.
Ecco 'l bell'erro c'ha da me a lei:
ch'i' non cherre' a Di' altro paradiso
che di basciar la terr' u' pon li piei;
ed i' fossi sicur d'un fiordaliso,
ch'ella dicesse: "Con vertà 'l ti diei" –
e no ch'i' fosse dal mondo diviso!

III

So little favour is in Becchina's mien,
I swear by God whose words no man can shake,
I know not where to turn or what to take;
Doctor and pills won't work, the pain's too keen.
More barbarous than a Saracen she's been,
Ay, worse than Herod was to baby Jews;
And yet I love her so much I'd refuse
To swap her if they offered me a queen.
Here lies my damning error to this hour,
To have asked no gift of Heaven but just to kiss
The dusty ground her feet have deigned to tread.
Now if she offered me a lily flower,
With: "Pray you, gentle sir, accept of this" –
Instead of which she says she wants me dead.

IV

Oimè d'Amor, che m'è duce sì reo,
oimè, che non potrebbe peggiorare;
oimè, perché m'avvene, segnor Deo?
Oimè, ch'i' amo quanto si pò amare,
oimè, colei che strugge lo cor meo!
Oimè, che non mi val mercé chiamare!
oimè, il su' cor com'è tanto giudeo,
oimè, che udir non mi vòl ricordare?
Oimè, quel punto maledetto sia,
oimè, ch'eo vidi lei cotanto bella,
oimè, ch'eo n'ho pure malinconia!
Oimè, che pare una rosa novella,
oimè, il su' viso: dunque villania,
oimè, cotanto come corre 'n ella?

IV

Alas, that Love's so bad a lord to obey;
Alas, no worse could any tyrant be!
Alas, my God, why does it happen to me?
Alas, to love as much as mortal may,
Alas, a wench who wears my heart away!
Alas, in vain I beg for clemency!
Alas, as fell as any Jew is she,
Alas, why won't she hear me named today?
Alas, a curse upon the time and place,
Alas, when I beheld her first so fair;
Alas, since then all joy has gone amiss!
Alas, a blushing rose was in her face:
Alas, who could have guessed she harboured there,
Alas indeed! barbarity like this?

V

Egli è sì agro il disamorare
a chi è 'nnamorato daddivero
che potrebb'anzi far del bianco nero
parer a quanti n'ha di qua da mare.
Ond'i', perciò, non vi vo' più pensare;
anzi, s'i' ebbi mai volere intero
in trasamar, or vi sarò più fèro:
portila Dio come la vuol portare!
Ma non l'abbia, perciò, in grad'Amore;
s'i' potesse, disamorar vorrìa
più volontier, che farmi 'mperadore:
ché tutto 'l tempo de la vita mia
so stato de' suo' servi servidore:
ed e' fammi pur mal, che Dio li dia!

V

To one who greatly cares, be it confessed,
So bitter is renouncing love that quite
As easy it would be to make all white
Men black throughout the countries of the West.
So I don't think of it with too much zest;
Even a love that gave me all my will
Would make me more intent on loving still:
Let God decide it then as suits him best.
But this confession Love shall not enjoy:
If well I could, the rogue I'd disavow,
Ay, rather than I'd wear the Imperial Crown.
Indeed, my lot, since I was just a boy,
Has been to wait upon his servants: now
If he would harm me more, God strike him down!

VI

Quanto un granel di panico è minore
del maggior monte che abbia veduto;
e quanto è 'l bon fiorin de l'or migliore
di qualunca denaro più minuto;
e quanto m'è più pessimo el dolore
ad averlo, e l'ho, ch'a averlo perduto:
cotant'è maggio la pena d'amore
ched io non averei mai creduto.
Ed or la credo, però ch'io la provo
en tal guisa che, per l'anima mia,
di questo amor vorrìa ancor esser novo.
Ed ho en disamar quella bailìa
c'ha 'l pulcinello ch'è dentro da l'ovo,
d'uscir 'nnanzi ched el su' tempo sia.

VI

By how much is a seed of millet less
Than is the highest mountain I behold,
By how much is a florin of fine gold
Worth more than some poor farthing's paltriness,
Even by how much is today's distress,
Felt more than any sorrow passed away;
By so much greater are the pangs, I say,
Of love than anything I once could guess.
But I believe it now: I've proved it true
To such extent that, for my very soul,
I wish my love were callow still and new.
To free myself today I've no more power
Than has the chick within its egg control
To hatch or not before the appointed hour.

VII

Io poterei così star senz'amore
come la soddomia tòllar a Moco,
o come Ciampolin gavazzatore
potesse vivar tollendoli 'l gioco,
o come Min di Pepo Accorridore
s'ardisse di toccar Tan pur un poco,
o come Migo, ch'è tutto d'errore,
ch'e' non morisse di caldo di fuoco.
Però mi facci Amor ciò che li piace,
ch'i' sarò sempre su' servo fedele
e sofferrò ciò che mi farà 'n pace;
e sed e' fosse amaro più che fele,
con l'umiltà ch'è vertù sì verace,
il farò dolce come cannamele.

VII

Deprived of love, I could no longer last
Than Moco with no boy to sodomize;
Or Ciampolino, holder of the prize
For prodigals, without the dice he casts,
Or Min di Pepo* who can run so fast
If he should challenge Tano just a little;
Or Migo if his heretic and brittle
Bones were delivered to the flames as lost.*
Yet Love shall do with me whate'er he will:
I'll serve him to the best of my ability,
Nor of his mastery will I complain;
And howsoever sharp his temper, still
With all the virtues of a pure humility,
I'll make him turn as sweet as sugarcane.

VIII

Quando veggio Becchina corrucciata,
se io avesse allor cuor di leone,
sì tremarei com'un picciol garzone
quando 'l maestro gli vuol dar palmata.
L'anima mia vorrebbe esser non nata,
'nanzi ch'aver cotale afflizïone;
e maledico el punto e la stagione
che tanta pena mi fu destinata.
Ma s'io devesse darmi a lo nemico,
e' si convien che io pur trovi la via
che io non temi el suo corruccio un fico.
Però, s'e' non bastasse, io mi morrìa;
ond'io non celo, anzi palese 'l dico,
ch'io provarò tutta mia valentìa.

VIII

When my Becchina's vexed and in a state,
Then even if I had a lion's heart,
I tremble like a schoolboy when he starts
To know the teacher's cane and fear its weight.
I'd rather not be born than aggravate
My soul with such a life of sore affliction:
I curse the hour with every malediction
That preordained me to my present fate.
I'd let the Devil take me, and declare
It well worthwhile, if thus I found a way
To snap my fingers at her angry mood.
But should that not suffice, then now I swear
To one and all that I intend to slay
Myself, and prove my courage unsubdued.

IX

Io averò quell'ora un sol dì bene,
ch'a Roma metterà neve d'agosto:
ma di dolor e d'angosce e di pene
son più fornito ca ottobre del mosto.
E solamente questo mal mi vene,
per ch'io non posso aver un buon risposto
da quella che 'l mie cor più tristo tene
che non fa quel che ne l'inferno è posto.
A torto e a peccato mi vòl male;
e così torni nostra guerra in pace
como di lei servir molto mi cale.
Così mi strugge stando contumace,
come ne l'acqua bollita fa 'l sale:
ch'io non n'ho peggio ancor, più li dispiace.

IX

I shall not see a single day that's fine
Till Rome lies buried under August snows;
But in the meantime I'm more rich in woes
Than is October with the must of wine.
For one cause only all this grief is mine:
Because I seek a kind reply, in vain,
From her who holds my heart in greater pain
Than damned souls ever got from wrath divine.
She has no cause to cause the pains I've felt,
And peace must follow war since, come what may,
I long to serve her, though she's so perverse.
Beneath her contumacious moods I melt
As salt in boiling water wastes away:
She's even sorry that I fare no worse.

X

La mia malinconia è tanta e tale
ch'i' non discredo che, s'egli 'l sapesse
un che mi fosse nemico mortale,
che di me di pietade non piangesse.
Quella per cu' m'avven, poco ne cale;
che mi potrebbe, sed ella volesse,
guarir 'n un punto di tutto 'l mie male
sed ella pur "I' t'odio" mi dicesse.
Ma quest'è la risposta c'ho da lei:
ched ella non mi vòl né mal né bene,
e ched i' vad'a far li fatti mei;
ch'ella non cura s'i' ho gioi' o pene
men ch'una paglia che le va tra' piei:
mal grado n'abbi Amor, ch'a le' mi diène.

X

My melancholy mood has grown so great
That now I really think that if my foe,
My mortal enemy, should chance to know,
He'd shed some pitying tears for my sad state.
While she who's quite indifferent to my fate,
Could even yet, if she were minded so,
Make perfect cure of all my present woe
By saying simply: "You're the one I hate!"
But no, she has one answer: that, in brief,
She wills me neither good nor evil now,
And hints I'd better mind my own affairs.
She troubles less if I have joy or grief,
Than for a straw she tramples on, I vow:
Accursed be Love who led me to these snares.

XI

E' m'è sì malamente rincresciuto
el pur amar e non essere amato,
che, come sasso, duro son tornato,
avvegna ch'a mal'otta sia pentuto.
E s'i' mi fosse anzi tratt'avveduto,
già non mi fuora sì caro costato,
ché ben n'ho men de la sangu'e del fiato,
e ne l'onor non me n'è guar cresciuto.
Sì che mi par aver bianca ragione
di non amar se non chi mi vòl bene,
ed in questo son fermo di piccone.
E chi altra manera prende o tene,
se non si cangia di su' oppinïone,
sarà fortuna se ben li n'avvene.

XI

So bitterly indeed have I lamented
To have kept loving when my love was spurned,
That like a heavy stone at last I'm turned,
Although too late I've probably repented.
Had I foreseen how I'd be discontented,
I might have bought such wisdom at less cost;
For while so much of blood and breath I've lost,
It's very sure my honour's not augmented.
But anyhow the moral's clear as day,
To love those only who are fond of me:
Henceforward in this view I'm firmly anchored.
And, for whoever thinks the other way
(Unless he changes quickly), it will be
A miracle if his whole life's not cankered.

XII

L'animo riposato aver solìa,
ed era nuovo che fosse dolore:
e or me n'ha così fornito Amore!
Non credo e penso ch'altra cosa sia.
Deh quant'è suta la sventura mia
poi ch'i' fu' servo di cotal segnore,
ché ciò ch'io faccio mi torna al peggiore
ver' quella che 'l me' cor ha 'n ubria.
Certo non me le par aver servito:
ché s'ella s'umiliass'a comandarmi,
non avrebbe ch'a levar lo su' dito.
Sì mi parrebbe poco trarriparmi,
potendo dir ch'i' l'avess'ubbidito;
s'i ne morisse, crederìe salvarmi.

XII

My mind has been accustomed to repose,
Indeed to trouble I am very new:
Is grief the guerdon Love provides? God knows
I've come to think no other plight is true.
So heavy has the burden of my woes
Grown since I first accepted Love as master,
That everything I do or I propose
To please my lady turns to my disaster.
I've surely served her now with all my might;
And if she deigned to give me some injunction,
A finger raised would serve as indication.
I'd go and take a leap from any height,
Proclaiming her command without compunction;
And if I died, I'd think it my salvation.

XIII

Il cuore in corpo mi sento tremare,
sì fort'è la temenza e la paura
ch'i' ho vedendo madonna in figura,
cotanto temo di lei innoiare.
E non porìa in quel punto parlare:
così mi si dà meno la natura
ched i' mi tengo in una gran ventura
quand'i' mi posso pur su' piei fidare.
Infino a tanto che non son passato,
tutti color che me veggiono andando
sì dicon: "Ve' colui, ch'è smemorato!"
Ed io nulla bestemmia lor ne mando,
ch'elli hanno le ragioni dal lor lato,
però che 'n ora in or vo tramazzando.

XIII

I feel my heart within my bosom beating,
So strong within me is the dread and fear,
Whenever I come face to face with her,
Lest she should be offended by our meeting.
Struck dumb am I, without a word of greeting,
And so alarmed that I might faint away,
I think myself most lucky, I must say,
If I don't topple over while retreating.
But as I stumble on like one possessed,
All those who see me marvel at the sight
And cry: "He's lost his wits, the crazy clown!"
I curse them not, I think restraint is best,
For reason certainly would say they're right,
And now and then, it's true, I tumble down.

XIV

Chi vòl vantaggio aver a l'altre genti
don'el su' cor lialmente ad Amore
e lassi dire amici né parenti,
s'e' n'ha nessun di ciò reprenditore:
che tanto faccia Dio tristi e dolenti
chi agli amanti fa altro ch'onore,
quant'elli ha fatto caràmpia, de denti,
che vintiquattro di bocca n'ha fuore.
Chi serve questa è peggio, a mia parvenza;
e ben mi par di ciò dicer sì certo,
che volentier ne starei a sentenza:
e chi perdesse, fosse sì deserto,
enmantinente, senza nulla entenza,
come fo 'l fiorentino a Monte Aperto.

XIV

Let him who would surpass his fellow men,
Give up his heart to Love in loyal guise,
And let his friends and kinsmen gossip then,
Should there be any prone to criticize.
To those who fail to honour lovers true
May God bring the same suffering and grief
As to some poor old woman who makes do
And eats without her four-and-twenty teeth.
But even worse off, so it seems to me,
Is one who serves a certain girl I've known;
I'll stake my life upon it that I'm right:
And let the one who's lost the wager be
Routed like those poor Florentines overthrown
When Montaperti* saw them put to flight.

XV

Amor, poi che 'n sì greve passo venni
che, chi vedìemi, ciascun dicìe: "Fiù!"
e di me beffe facìen maggior più
ch'i' dir non so, schernendomi per cenni,
era sì fuor di tutti e cinque senni
ch'a 'maginar quanto 'n tutt'era giù
d'ogn'intelletto, ch'om di' aver chiù,
sarìa lament', e a pensar du' m'attenni
ch'i' non perìo; ma al tu' gentil soccorso
che mi donasti quand'i' venìe meno
ciascun membro gridò: "No' sbigottiamo!"
Di guiderdon ma' non potre' aver ramo
ch'i' renderti potesse; ma tal freno
m'hai messo 'n bocca che mai non lo smorso.

XV

Love, when you brought me down to such a state
That everyone who saw me started mocking,
With oohs and ahs, holding their sides and rocking
With gestures that I'd rather not relate,
To my five senses I was so far lost
That it would be a sorry tale to tell
How I declined in intellect as well,
The one thing that a poor man needs the most
In order to survive. Then came the aid
You offered me when I was like to die,
Though every nerve was crying out with terror.
And now, though what I owe you can't be paid,
You've put a bit between my teeth, and I
Champ on it, knowing that it's there for ever.

XVI

L'Amor, che m'è guerrero ed enemico,
m'ha fatto com'al drago san Michele,
e mi fa canne somigliar candele:
guarda s'i' son ben di veder mendico.
Garzon di tempo e di savere antico,
fui già chiamato fonte di cautele;
ma veramente come Cristo 'n ciel è,
i' son del tutto folle, e nol disdico.
Però chi mi riprende di fallare,
nol mir'a dritto specchi', al mi' parere:
ché contra forza senno suol perire.
E non per tanto, ché del migliorare
non si sa punt', anz'i' potre' morire –
dica chi vuol, ch'i' 'l mett'a non calere.

XVI

Now Love makes war on me, my deadliest foe;
Like Satan by Saint Michael, I'm defeated;
Now I take canes for candles; thus I'm treated;
I can't see straight. Don't say it isn't so.
A likely learnèd lad not long ago,
Men counted me a prudent paragon,
But now, as sure as heaven's where Christ has gone,
I've gone stark mad, as far too well I know.
And yet all those who blame me as unwise
Should find a clearer glass where they would see
How force alone suppresses wisdom there.
But where the cure for this distemper lies
No man can tell; unless it's Death maybe:
Say what you like, for I no longer care.

XVII

Quand'i' solev'udir ch'un fiorentino
si fosse per dolor sì disperato
ched elli stesso si fosse 'mpiccato,
sì mi parev'un miracol divino;
ed or m'è viso che sie più latino
che non sarebb'a un che, solo nato,
avesse tutto 'l dì marmo segato,
il bever un becchier di vernaccino.
Perciò ch'i' ho provat'un tal dolore
ch'i' credo che la pena de la morte
sia cento milia cotanto minore.
Com'elli sia così pessim'e forte,
come 'l sonetto dic'e vie maggiore,
farò parer con men di due ritorte.

XVII

Whenever I was told a Florentine,
Egged on by anguish into desperation,
Had hanged himself beyond reanimation,
I saw it as a miracle divine;
But now it seems as natural and in line
As that some marble-cutter, passing by
After the dusty day that leaves him dry,
Should ease his gullet with a cup of wine.
For since I've borne with such unhappiness,
I feel the pangs of death are surely less,
Less by a thousand times. So I'll not palter.
I'll prove at once how great is my despair,
Far greater than this sonnet can declare,
By means of nothing but a simple halter.

XVIII

Se si potesse morir di dolore,
molti son vivi che serebber morti –
i' son l'un desso, s'e' non me ne porti
'n anim'e carn' il Lucifer maggiore;
avvegna ch'i' ne vo con la peggiore,
ché ne lo 'nferno non son così forti
le pene e li tormenti e li sconforti
com'un de' miei, qualunqu'è 'l minore.
Ond'io esser non nato ben vorrìa,
od esser cosa che non si sentisse,
poi ch'i' non trovo 'n me modo né via,
se non è 'n tanto che se si compisse
per avventura omai la profezia,
che l'uom vuol dir che Anticristo venisse.

XVIII

If it were possible mere grief could slay,
How many are now alive who would be dead:
Myself for one, since Lucifer the Dread
Forbears to snatch me body and soul away.
Not that my sufferings are less, I say,
For hell contains no punishment so dire,
No pangs of tribulation in the fire,
Compared with all I undergo today.
Therefore I wish that I had not been born,
Or born a thing unfeeling, since of late
I find no way to lessen sorrow's sum.
And being in this manner most forlorn,
I'd welcome the arrival of the date,
So long foretold, when Antichrist should come.

XIX

Eo ho sì tristo il cor di cose cento,
che cento – volte el dì penso morire,
avvegna che 'l morir – mi fora abento,
ch'eo non ho abento – se non di dormire;
e nel dormir – ho tanto di tormento,
che di tormento – non posso guarire;
ma ben guarir – porìa en un momento,
se un momento – avesse quella che ire
mi fa tanto dolente, en fede mia,
che mia – non par che sia alcuna cosa,
altro che cosa – corrucciosa e ria.
Ed è si ria – la mia vita dogliosa,
ch'eo so doglios'a – chi mi scontra en via;
e via – non veggio che mai aggia posa.

XIX

My heart's so weighted with a hundred woes,
A hundred times a day death comes in sight;
Though death at least would offer me some rest,
Who have no rest save when I sleep at night;
But sleep's so full of torment, Heaven knows,
That torment seems incurable, yet I
Would find a cure that moment, if she chose
A moment to relent; she makes me sigh,
But sigh indeed I must; for, truth to say,
There's truth in nothing of this world's abode,
Except things that are evil, changing never;
And evil is my life, its sorrowing road,
In sorrow I see travellers on the way,
But see no way to any respite ever.*

XX

Me' mi so cattiveggiar su 'n un letto
che neun om che vada 'n su' duo piei:
ché 'n prima fo degli altru' danar miei;
or udirete po' com'i' m'assetto:
ché 'n una cheggio, per maggior diletto,
d'essere in braccio 'n braccio con colei
a cu' l'anim'e 'l cuor e 'l corpo diei
interamente, senz'alcun difetto.
Ma po' ched i' mi trovo 'n sul nïente
di queste cose ch'i' m'ho millantato,
fo mille morti 'l dì, sì son dolente.
E tutto 'l sangue mi sento turbato,
ed ho men posa che l'acqua corrente –
ed avrò fin ch'i' sarò 'nnamorato.

XX

Of how to while the time in bed away
I know a better mode than many a man:
But first it's clear that someone else must pay;
Now you shall hear the measure of my plan:
With cash in hand, I'd ask, for more delight,
To have the one I love and pay my due,
Locked arm-in-arm, spending without respite,
Giving my soul and heart and body too.
But since, alas! I find myself without
The very things I used to boast about,
Each day I die a thousand deaths in vain.
My very blood is boiling in my breast,
And, like a waterfall, I have no rest,
Nor shall I have till love has cooled again.

XXI

Da po' t'è 'n grado, Becchina, ch'i' muoia,
non piacci a Dio ch'i' viva nïente!
Anima mia, morir ben m'è a puoia,
per allegrezza di quel tu' parente
c'ha nome Benci, che pela le coia;
però ti dico ch'i' moio dolente;
ma non però ch'i' ne cur'una luoia,
anzi ne prego Crist'onnipotente
ch'e' ne contenti 'l mie bocì'al bosco;
ché so che m'odian di sì crudel guisa
che di vedermi morto menan tòsco!
Mit'e Turella ne farà gran risa,
Nell'e Pogges'e tutti que' del cosco,
accetto que' che fuor nati di Pisa.

XXI

Since on my death, Becchina, you are bent,
Let God the consummation not retard!
Yet, by my very soul, I find it hard,
For it will give your father great content.
To think of Skinner Benci's* merriment
Makes dying doubly irksome, even if
For actual death I could not spare a sniff;
Indeed, I pray to Christ omnipotent
That he will grant the wish; for some, it's said,
Are now so very keen to see me dead,
Their spittle turns to poison in their spite.
Tura and Mit will laugh and fall in fits,
Nello and all my kin be thrilled to bits,
Save those of Pisan birth, if I know right.

XXII

"Becchina mia!" – "Cecco, nol ti confesso."
"Ed i'son tu'." – "E cotesto disdico."
"I' sarò altrui." – "Non vi do un fico."
"Torto mi fai." – "E tu mi manda 'l messo."
"Sì, maccherella." – "Ell'avrà 'l capo fesso."
"Chi gliele fenderae?" – "Ciò ti dico."
"Se' così niffa?" – "Sì, contra 'l nimico."
"Non tocc'a me." – "Anzi, pur tu se' desso."
"E tu t'ascondi." – "E tu va' col malanno."
"Tu non vorresti." – "Perché non vorrìa?"
"Ché se' pietosa." – "Non di te, uguanno!"
"Se foss'un altro?" – "Cavere'l d'affanno."
"Mal ti conobbi!" – "Or non di' tu bugia."
"Non me ne poss'atar." – "Abbieti 'l danno!"

XXII

"Becchina mine!" – "Cecco, that isn't true."
"At least I'm yours." – "A falsehood just as big."
"I'll be another's." – "I don't care a fig."
"You wrong me." – "Send a lawyer, say you'll sue."
"I'll send some bawd." – "I'll crack her head in two."
"Who'll crack her head?" – "I've told you, now you know."
"Are you so waspish?" – "Yes, against a foe."
"You don't mean me." – "Make no mistake, I do."
"You're hiding something." – "Take my curse and go."
"You can't wish that." – "Indeed, why shouldn't I?"
"Because you're kind." – "This year I'm something new."
"If I were someone else?" – "I'd cure his woe."
"Alas, how I've misjudged you!" – "Do not lie."
"I can't defend myself." – "Too bad for you!"

XXIII

E' non è neun con cotanto male,
che volontier non li cambiasse stato,
però ch'el me' dolor è sì corale,
che passa quel d'ogn'altro sciagurato;
ché, per segarmi la vena organale,
quella di cu' i' sono innamorato
darebbevi più che rusca non vale:
a questo m'ha condutto el mio peccato.
Ch'ella sempre dice, ha ditto e cre' dica,
difin che dicerò di lei amare,
d'essermi pure mortale nemica;
là 'nd'eo ne porto en me tanto penare.
Se Dëo, ch'è segnor, mi benedica,
e' darìa gli occhi per disamorare.

XXIII

There's nobody who would not change his state,
Smitten the way I am; though now, alas,
My load of sorrow has become so great,
All other wretches' grief it must surpass.
And if this cruel lady saw me slice
My jugular vein, she'd take it coolly too,
She wouldn't need to think about it twice:
And this is what my sin has brought me to.
She says, has said, and I believe will say
That just so long as I tell her my love,
She's bound to stay my mortal enemy.
Wherefore I bear such agonies today,
That if God blessed the deed from heaven above,
I'd give my very eyeballs to be free.

XXIV

Lo mi' cor non s'allegra di covelle,
ch'i' veggia o ch'i' oda ricordare;
anzi mi fa, non ch'altro, noia l'âre,
tal'odo da mia donna le novelle;
ché 'nsomm'ha detto ch'aver de le stelle
potre' innanzi che lei accordare
ched ella si volesse umilïare
ch'i' l'appressass'al suol de le pianelle.
Onde la morte mi sarebbe vita,
ed i' vorre' morir trasvolontieri,
ché me' val una morte far che mille.
Or va', sonetto, a la mia donna, e dille
che s'i' potesse retornar en ieri
io la farei grattar con diece dita.

XXIV

Today no joy unto my heart accrues
From all I see and hear on every side;
The very air I breathe I scarce abide,
Since from my lady comes such evil news.
In short, these seem to be her present views:
I'll sooner have the stars within my clutch
Than she'll demean herself to let me touch
The leather soles upon her dainty shoes.
Then surely death were life to such as I,
Wherefore most willingly at once I'd die,
One pang being better than a doom that lingers.
Now go, my sonnet, to my mistress say
That could I but revert to yesterday,
I'd scratch her up and down with my ten fingers.

XXV

Sonetto, da poi ch'i' non trovo messo
che vad'a quella che 'l me' cor disìa,
merzé, per Dio! or mi vi va' tu stesso
da la mia parte, sì che bene istia;
e dille ca d'amor so' morto adesso,
se non m'aiuta la sua cortesia;
e quando tu le parli, istà di cesso,
ch'i ho d'ogni persona gelosia.
Se mi degnasse volerm'a servente,
anche non mi si faccia tanto bene,
promettile per me sicuramente
che ciò ch'a la gentile si convene,
io 'l farò di bon cor, sì lealmente,
ch'ella averà pietà de le mie pene.

XXV

My sonnet, since no messenger I find
To approach the lady of my heart's desire,
I bless the Lord that you are so inclined,
No fitter deputy could I require:
Tell her my love, and how I must expire,
Unless she helps me, courteous and kind;
But while you're talking, keep your distance, mind,
Or jealousy will set me soon on fire.
And if she deigns to use me as a servant,
Although it's not the role that I prefer,
Then promise her sincerely for my part
That, in all necessary things observant,
I'll work so loyally at pleasing her
That she'll take pity on my suffering heart.

XXVI

Anima mia, cuor del mi' corp', amore,
alquanto di merzé e pietà ti prenda
di me, che vivo 'n cotanto dolore
che 'n ora 'n ora par che 'l cuor mi fenda
per la gran pena ch'i' ho del tremore
ched i' non t'abbi anzi che porti benda;
sed i' ne muoio, non ti sarà onore:
se vorra' puo', non potra' far l'ammenda.
Avvegna ch'i' non sia degno trovare
in te merzé, pietà né cortesia,
nïente men lassarò di pregare:
però ch'Amor comand'e vòl che sia
licita cosa di poter amare
in quella donna che 'l su' cor disìa.

XXVI

Soul of my soul, heart of my flesh, I plead
That in your breast some pity might awake;
I live in so much sorrow that indeed
I fear that any hour my heart will break
With fear to see the bridal fillet bind
Your brow before I have you. Don't depend
On being honoured in my death; you'll find
That when you want to, you can't make amends.
Yet even if I'm judged unfit to claim
Your courtesy or pity or compassion,
I'll still keep pleading, and will never tire.
For Love itself dictates and wills the same,
And holds it as a fair and lawful fashion
To enjoy the lady that your heart desires.

XXVII

"Oncia di carne, libra di malizia,
per che dimostri quel che 'n cor non hai?"
"Se' tu sì pazzo ch'aspetti divizia
di quel che caramente comparrai?"
"Per tue parole 'l me' cor non affizia;
com peggio dici, più speme mi dai!"
"Credi che uom aggia mai la primizia?
Giùroti 'n fede mia che non avrai."
"Or veggio ben che tu caschi d'amore:
per che non muove ciò che tu ha' detto
se non da cuor ch'è forte 'nnamorato."
"Or vuo' pur esser con cotest'errore?
Or vi sta' sempre, che sie benedetto!
ch'i' ti 'mprometto…" – "…Che 'l buon dì m'ha'dato."

XXVII

"An ounce of flesh for every pound of spite,
Your heart can't mean all that your words declare."
"Are you so mad to think I mean to share
What I have bought so dear and hold so tight?"
"Say what you like: be sure I won't take fright;
As you grow fierce, my hope becomes more fair."
"You think you'll pluck my first-fruit? No, I swear,
That's one thing you won't get: it isn't right."
"I see it's love that causes your confusion,
For every sentiment that you've expressed
Springs from a heart already passion-sore."
"And so you want to stick to this delusion?
Then do so now and always be blessed!
I promise this…" – "And you showed me the door."

XXVIII

Se 'l cor di Becchina fosse diamante
e tutta l'altra persona d'acciaio,
e fosse fredda com'è di gennaio
in quella part' u' non può 'l sol levante;
ed ancor fosse nata d'un giogante,
sì com'ell'è d'un agevol coiaio,
ed i' foss'un che toccasse 'l somaio,
non mi dovrebbe dar pene cotante.
Ma s'ell'un poco mi stess'a udita
ed i' avesse l'ardir di parlare,
credo che fora mia speme compita:
ch'i' le dire' com'i' son su' a vita,
e altre cose ch'or non vo' contare;
parm'esser certo ch'ella direbb' "ita".

XXVIII

If diamond-hard were my Becchina's heart,
And all the rest of her were made of steel,
And if she were as cold as is the feel
Of January in some sunless part:
Were she the daughter of a giant, say,
Not of a tanner, quietest of men,
And I muleteer, why even then
I'd suffer less on her account today.
Yet if she chose to listen to me now,
While I explained more boldly my intention,
I fancy all might end in happiness:
That I am hers for life at once I'd vow,
With other matters I forbear to mention,
To which I'm pretty sure she'd answer "Yes".

XXIX

Se tutta l'acqu'a balsamo tornasse
e la terr'òr diventasse a carrate,
e tutte queste cose mi donasse
quel che n'avrebbe ben la podestate,
per che mia donna del mondo passasse,
e' li dicerei: "Misser, or l'abbiate!"
ed anzi ch'al partito m'accordasse
sosterrei dura morte, en veritate.
Ché solamente du' o pur tre capegli
contra sua voglia non vorrei l'uscisse,
per caricar d'oro mille camegli.
Ma i' vorrei ched ella mel credesse –
ché tante maitinate e tanti svegli,
come li fo, non credo ch'e' perdesse.

XXIX

If God should change the water in the sea
To precious balm, and all the land to gold,
And if, as he well could, he offered me
All this for ever, mine to have and hold,
On one condition, that my lady be
Rapt from the world, I'd say: "No thanks, Sir, you
Can keep the lot." For rather than agree,
I'd suffer horrid death, and this is true.
I wouldn't sell two hairs from her sweet head
Against her will, not if the gold they'd bring
Would burden thousands in a camel train.
I hope she will believe what I have said,
For then the songs to her that I still sing
At dawn and dusk will not have been in vain.

XXX

Figliuol di Dio, quanto ben avre' avuto
se la mia donna m'avesse degnato
di volermi per schiavo ricomprato,
come colui ch'a lo port'è venduto!
Me dolente, a le cu' man son caduto! –
ch'oggi giurò su ne l'altar sagrato
che s'ella mi vedesse strascinato
non dicerebbe: "Che è quello issuto?"
Ma Amor ne sie con le', s'elli 'l può fare,
ché ma' questa speranza non mi tolle,
che 'l canto non mi torni 'n sufolare.
S'ella m'odiasse quanto Siena Colle,
sì mi pur credo tanto umilïare
che 'l su' cor duro ver' del mi' fi' molle.

XXX

O Son of God, how blessed would be my state,
If my dear lady were content to buy
Me for her slave, like those sold wretches I
See on the quayside where they stand and wait.
Alas, in what fell hands I've fallen of late!
Indeed, I'd swear upon the sacred altar
That if she saw me dragged past by a halter,
She wouldn't ask "How did he meet his fate?"
But yet Love will not leave her to her ease,
For nothing can remove this hope, my dream,
That soon I won't sing sad, but whistle often.
And though she hates me as the Sienese
Do those of Colle,* I'll so humble seem
That even her hard heart will start to soften.

XXXI

I' ho sì gran paura di fallare
verso la dolce gentil donna mia
ch'i' non l'ardisco la gioia domandare
che 'l mi' coraggio cotanto disìa;
ma 'l cor mi dice pur d'assicurare,
per che 'n lei sento tanta cortesia
ch'eo non potre' quel dicere né fare
ch'i' adirasse la sua segnoria.
Ma se la mia ventura mi consente
ch'ella mi degni di farmi quel dono,
sovr'ogn'amante viverò gaudente.
Or va', sonetto, e chiedile perdono
s'io dico cosa che le sia spiacente:
ché, s'io non l'ho, già mai lieto non sono.

XXXI

My dread becomes so great lest I should err
Toward the lady that my heart desires,
That I lack courage to request of her
The joy to which my passion now aspires.
Even my heart still warns me to refrain,
For such high courtesy within her lies,
That, without insult, I could not explain
Such things before her sweet seigneurial eyes.
But should my luck and wishes once agree
So that she deigned to grant me this great treasure,
I'd be the happiest of lovers then.
Now, sonnet, go: ask her to pardon me,
If I've said anything to cause displeasure;
For if she won't, I'll never smile again.

XXXII

"Deh, bàstat'oggimai, per cortesia,
in verità, ché tutt'ha bel posare!"
"Certo, amore, così far lo porìa,
come galluccio potesse volare."
"Tu mi fara' venir tal bizzarria,
qual i' mi so, puo' che così de' andare."
"Perché dici così, anima mia?
ha' voglia ch i' mi vad'a trarripare?"
"Volesse Dio che tu fossi già mosso –
ch'assa' mi piacerìa cotal novella,
da poi che rimaner far non ti posso."
"Or, s' tu fossi pietosa come bella,
se 'l mi' penser non m'inganna di grosso,
de la persona tua diresti: 'Tèlla!'"

XXXII

"I pray you cease, in courtesy comply,
For all is settled now as it should be!"
"Of course, my love, and you can count on me
When you expect the barnyard cocks to fly."
"You'll really put it in my head to go
In some such giddy way, and bid goodbye."
"Why say you thus, my soul? You wish that I
Should find some cliff and plunge headfirst below?"
"Would God you were already gone! I swear
That news of it would leave me much relieved,
Who've neither will nor power to make you stay."
"Now if you were as kind as you are fair,
Unless my understanding be deceived,
You'd stand and tell me, 'Yours to take away!'"

XXXIII

Io son sì altamente innamorato,
a la mercé d'una donna e d'Amore,
ch'e' non è al mondo re né imperadore
a cui volessi io già cambiar mio stato:
ch'io amo quella a cui Dio ha donato
tutto ciò che conviene a gentil core;
dunque, chi di tal donna è servidore
ben si può dir che 'n buon pianeto è nato.
Ed ella ha 'l cor tanto cortese e piano
inver' di me, la mia gentile manza,
che, sua mercé, basciata li ho la mano.
E sì mi diè ancor ferma speranza
che di qui a poco, se Dio mi fa sano,
io compierò di lie' mia disïanza.

XXXIII

I am indeed so much in love today,
Thanks to my lady and the god Amor,
That not with any king or emperor
I'd barter such a blessed state away;
For God above has chosen to display
All virtues of the gentle heart* in her;
Thus one who serves such grace may well aver
His birth beneath some lucky planet's ray.
So kind and courteous she's become to me
That she has gone so far as to permit
That I should kiss her hand without demur.
And thus again, a firm-based hope I see
That before long, if the Lord keeps me fit,
I'll satisfy my great desire for her.

XXXIV

I' ho tutte le cose ch'io non voglio,
e non ho punto di quel che mi piace,
poi ch'io non trovo con Becchina pace;
là 'nd'io ne porto tutto 'l mio cordoglio,
che non caprebbe, scritto, su 'n un foglio
che gli fuss'entro la Bibbia capace:
ch'io ardo come foco in la fornace,
membrando quel che da lei aver soglio;
ché le stelle del cielo non son tante,
ancora ch'io torrei esser digiuno,
quanti baci li die' in un istante
in me' la bocca, ed altro uom nessuno:
e fu di giugno vinti dì a l'intrante,
anni mille dugento novantuno.

XXXIV

That I have everything I don't desire,
And nothing that I do, there's not a doubt;
All since Becchina and myself fell out:
And now my grief assumes proportions dire,
So that the writing of it would require
More parchment than the Bible, God forgive me!
For when I think of what she used to give me,
There is no furnace burning like my fire.
More kisses than the stars in heaven above
(Though now I wish that I had starved my ardour)
I rained upon her mouth, faster and harder
Than any man who ever was in love.
The twentieth day of June that prize I won,
And the year was twelve hundred ninety-one.

XXXV

Per ogne gocciola d'acqua c'ha 'n mare,
ha cento mili' allegrezze 'l meo core,
e qualunqu'è di tutte la minore
procura più ch'a' romani 'l Sudare;
ch'i' seppi tanto tra dicere e fare
ched i' sali' su l'àlbor de l'Amore,
ed a la sua mercé colsi quel fiore
ch'io tanto disïava d'odorare.
E po' ch'i' fu' di quell'albero sceso,
sì volsi per lo frutto risalire:
ma non poteo, però ch'i' fu' conteso.
Ma gir mi vo' chel fior, ch'i' ho, a gioire,
ch'assa' di volte 'n proverbio l'ho 'nteso:
chi tutto vuole, nulla de' avire.

XXXV

For every drop of water in the sea
A hundred thousand joys are in my heart,
The least of which more pleasure brings to me
Than does the Holy Veil to Rome impart.*
Between the word and deed is many a slip,
And so the Tree of Love I sought to climb,
And there the flower I was given to clip
That I had longed to smell for such a time.
Once on the ground and from the tree descended,
I thought to go back up and pluck the fruit,
But found I could not do as I intended.
Still I enjoy the flower as worth pursuit,
For oftentimes the proverb I recall:
He ends with nothing who sets out for all.

XXXVI

S'i' non torni ne l'odïo d'Amore,
che non vorre' per aver Paradiso:
i' ho 'n tal donna lo mi' cor assiso,
che, chi dicesse "Ti fo 'mperadore,
e sta' che non la veggi pur du' ore"
sì li direi: "Va', che sii ucciso!"
ed in vedendo lei sì son diviso
da tutto quel che si chiama dolore.
Avvegna ch'i' di ciò me n'ho mistiere
di veder cosa che dolor mi tolla:
ch'è più quel che mi fa frat'Angioliere
che per mille ore stare 'n su la colla;
che già diece anni li rupp'un bicchiere:
ancor di maladìciarmi non molla.

XXXVI

Unless I risk Love's enmity once more
(A thing I wouldn't do to save my soul),
My lady has my heart so firm and whole
That if one said "I'll crown you Emperor
When you agree to do without her for
Two hours, that's all", I'd cry "Let him be slain!"
In sight of her I'm free from present pain
And all remembered pangs I've felt before.
But though I've this advantage here below
That I may look on one of healing powers,
At times Friar Angiolieri* damns me so,
It's like being strung up for a thousand hours:
I broke a glass of his ten years ago,
And still his curses fall on me in showers.

XXXVII

Qualunque ben si fa, naturalmente
nasce d'Amor, come del fiore el frutto,
ché Amor fa l'omo essere valente;
ancor fa più ch'e' nol trova sì brutto
che per lui non si adorni a mantinente,
e non par esso poi, sì 'l muta tutto;
dunque po' dicer bene veramente:
che chi non ama sia morto e distrutto.
Ch'omo val tanto quanto in sé ha bontate,
e la bontà senza Amor non pò stare:
dunque ben ho eo usato vertate.
Or va', sonetto, senza dimorare
a tutti innamorati e innamorate,
e di' lor che Becchina ti fa fare.

XXXVII

Surely of Love all natural good is born
Even as fruit must be the child of flower,
For Love emboldens all men with his power;
Indeed, there's no man that he holds in scorn,
No man so vile that he will not adorn,
Ennoble and transform in one brief hour;
And thus we say the scoffing wretch and sour
Who will not love should be in pieces torn.
A man is worth what good within him lies,
And goodness without Love most surely dies;
Which means that good is what my heart desired.
Now go, my sonnet, and make no delay,
To every loving man and maiden say
That by Becchina you have been inspired.

XXXVIII

Chi non sente d'Amor o tant'o quanto
in tutt'i tempi che vita li dura,
così de' esser sotterrat'a santo
come colui che non rendé l'usura:
ed e' medesmo si pò dare un vanto
che Dio co' santi l'odia oltre misura.
Ma qual è que' che d'Amor porta manto,
e' pò ben dir che gli è pretta ventura;
però ch'Amor è sì nobile cosa
che, s'elli entrasse 'n colu' de lo 'nferno
che non ebb'anch'e non dé' aver posa,
pena non sentìrebbe 'n sempiterno:
la vita sua sarìa più gioïosa
che non rubaldo a l'uscita del verno.

XXXVIII

The man who feels no power of Love pervade
All seasons of his life on earth should be
Denied church-burial like one that's made
No restitution for his usury:
And such a man can boast aloud that he
Is loathed by God and all the saints above;
While he that wears the livery of love
May vaunt himself in luck assuredly.
For Love is such a very noble thing
That if it entered in the Devil's breast,
Where never was nor ever should be rest,
Those hellish pains would be for ever gone:
Within his heart a greater joy would spring
Than in a beggar's when the winter's done.

XXXIX

"Becchin'amore, i' ti solev'odiare
a rispetto ch'i' t'am'or di buon cuore."
"Cecco, s'i mi potesse 'n te fidare,
el mie cuor fuora di te servidore."
"Becchin'amore, piacciati provare
sed i' ti son leal o traditore."
"Cecco, ...
...."
"Becchin'amore, or veggio certamente
che tu non vuo' ched i' servir ti possa,
da puo' che mi comandi 'l non possente."
"Cecco, l'umiltà tua m'ha sì rimossa
che giamma' ben né gioia 'l mie cor sente,
se di te nove mesi non vo grossa."

XXXIX

"Becchina dear, I hated you before,
Compared with how I deeply love today."
"Cecco, could I believe in what you say,
My heart would be your servant evermore."
"Becchina dear, to prove how I adore
You with a loyal heart, what should I try?"
"Cecco, ...
...."*
"Becchina dear, most clearly now I see
That you don't want my service; I should go,
Since you demand what nobody could do."
"Cecco, I'm touched by your humility
So much that happiness I'll never know
Until I'm nine months big with child by you."

XL

Sed i' avess'un sacco di fiorini
e non ve n'avess'altro che de' nuovi,
e fosse mi' Arcidoss'e Montegiuovi
con cinquicento some d'aquilini,
non mi parrì' aver tre bagattini
senza Becchin' – or dunque, 'n che ti provi,
babbo, di gastigarm'! Or ché non movi
de la lor fede tutti saracini?
E potrest'anzi, s'i' non sia ucciso –
per ch'i' son fermo 'n quest'uppinïone:
ched ella sia un terren paradiso.
E vòtene mostrar viva ragione
che ciò sia vero: chi la sguarda 'n viso,
sed egli è vecchio, ritorna garzone.

XL

If I had loads of florins in a sack,
And every one of them was shining new,
And Arcidosso and Montegiovi* too,
And silver Pisan coins in many a pack,
I still would feel a pauper for the lack
Of my Becchina. And so what's the good
Of blaming me, Dad? Don't you think you should
Convert the Saracens and get off my back?
And if that isn't easier, strike me dead:
But nothing can unsettle what I've said,
That she's an earthly paradise in truth.
Moreover I can prove this is the case,
For any man who looks into her face,
However old he is, regains his youth.

XLI

Io poterei così disamorare
come veder Ficecchio da Bologna
o l'Indïa maggior di val di Pogna
o de la val di Bocchezzan lo mare,
o a mie posta veder lo Sudare,
o far villan uom che tema vergogna,
o tutto 'nterpetrare ciò ch'uom sogna,
o cosa fatta poter istornare.
Dunqua che val s'i' ne son gastigato?
Ché, se non vien dal cuor, sì val nïente:
da crédarm'è, tanto l'aggio provato.
Chi mi riprende non sa 'l convenente,
ch'allora mi 'ncende 'l cor d'ogni lato,
e per un mille vi son più fervente.

XLI

To give up Love would be as hard for me
As to make out Fucecchio from Bologna,
Descry the Indies from the Val di Pogna,
Or glance from Boccheggiano* to the sea;
Or see the Holy Veil from here maybe,
Or fill a rogue with shame's humiliation,
Or give men's dreams their true interpretation,
Or change the past and alter Time's decree.
So what's the point of taking me aside
And blaming me? For when the heart says no,
It can't be done: believe me I have tried.
Those who rebuke me really ought to know
They only stoke the fire on every side
That burns a thousand times more brightly so.

XLII

La mïa donna m'ha mandato un messo
ch'i'non lasci per nulla ch'i' non vada
a lëi per la più diritta strada
che io posso, conservando me stesso;
e dice che li batte el cuor sì spesso
che, 'nanzi che questo giorno ne vada,
morrà, di me così forte l'aggrada
e non del dì, per veder s'i' son esso!
Ecco novelle che mi son recate!
E vedete, signor, s'i' 'l posso fare,
ché son lungi a lei ben tre giornate.
Caval non ho – a piè non posso andare
quattro miglia per dì: l'abbo, pensate!
Signor, vedete s'i' la posso aitare.

XLII

My Lady's sent a messenger here to me,
To say that I should come without delay,
By the directest route that I can see,
And reach her, sound of limb, as best I may.
She says her heart so trembles in her breast
That by tonight she'll surely pass away;
That love for me has made her so distressed
And I must prove my worth this very day.
Such is the news that just has come to hand!
Imagine, Sir, what I'm supposed to do:
It's three days' journey, you will understand,
And I've no horse; and one thing more is true,
I can't walk four miles in a day. Yet now
I'd have her, think of it! Just tell me how.

XLIII

Sed i' avess'un mi' mortal nemico
ed i' 'l vedesse 'n segnoria d'Amore,
in su quel caso li tornere' amico
e servire'l sì come mio segnore;
e ch'i' altro facesse, il contraddico,
però ch'i' ho provato quel dolore –
chéd esser ricch'e divenir mendico
è appo quell'un farsi 'mperadore.
Chi nol mi crede, sì'l possa provare
sì come io, che per lo mio peccato
cinqu'anni ho tempestato 'n su quel mare.
E quand'i' credev'esser apportato,
una corrente ch'è peggio che 'l Fare
sì m'intravers' – e pur son arrestato.

XLIII

Now if I chanced to have a mortal foe
And I beheld him subject to Love's law,
He'd then become my friend, I'd treat him so,
And serve him as my lord for evermore.
Could I do otherwise? Let it not be said!
I've suffered all those torments, one by one:
The man once rich who now must beg his bread
Would seem an emperor in comparison.
To those incredulous I would retort:
Bear what I've borne, and to my bitter shame,
The five long years I tossed on passion's sea.
And when at last I hoped to reach the port,
Worse than Messina Straits,* a current came
And swept me back, and still it baffles me.

XLIV

Il come né 'l perché ben lo sa Dio:
in neun modo veder i' non posso
per ch'a Becchina sia 'l cuore rimosso,
ch'essar solev'una cosa col mio;
ed or non ha più speme né disio
che di vedermi tranat'ad un fosso;
e 'l diavol m'ha di le' fatto sì grosso
che metter già non la posso 'n ubblìo.
Credo che sia per alcun mi' peccato
che Die mi vuol questo pericol dare,
per ched i' l'am'e da le' si' odiato.
E s'or un tempo m'ha lasciat'andare,
s'i' veggio 'l dì ch'i' sia disamorato,
saprò un poc'allor più che mi fare.

XLIV

Not even God himself in heaven can know,
Much less can I in any way divine,
Why my Becchina's heart has altered so,
That used to beat in unison with mine.
Her one desire is that someone throw
Me in a common grave, already rotten,
Yet still the Devil, prowling here below,
Makes sure that in my heart she's not forgotten.
I think this penance has been laid on me,
Because of certain sins, by God above,
That I should long for one who wants me dead.
Yet since, for a short time, he left me free,
I hope one day I may be cured of love,
And better know the road that I shall tread.

XLV

Se io potesse con la lingua dire
la minor pena ch'io sento d'Amore,
e la mia donna lo degnasse udire,
s'ella fosse del mondo la piggiore,
io non son sì sicuro del morire
ch'i' non son più del suo spietato core:
farebbe tutto quel che m'ho 'n desire,
odiendomi contar tanto dolore.
Volentier tornerì' a sua segnoria
se 'l mio servir le fosse in piacimento;
ma io so bene ch'ella non vorrìa,
ch'io n'ho udito questo in saramento:
quando io vo in parte dove sia,
fugge, per non vedermi, come 'l vento.

XLV

Now if I had the words that could rehearse
The least of all the pains Love makes me bear,
And if, at last, my lady deigned to hear,
Although no woman in the world were worse;
Though I'm less certain of my death, I swear,
Than I'm convinced that she is pitiless,
I think she'd grant all my desires success
For weariness at hearing my despair.
Indeed, I'd serve her still, if I knew how
To make that service pleasing to her eyes;
But well I know that she would not agree,
I'm told she swore it with a solemn vow.
When I come round, she's off, away she flies;
Gone with the wind rather than look on me.

XLVI

E' fu già tempo che Becchina m'era
di sì buon âre ch'i' era contento,
né avre' chesto più mar né più vento,
tant'allegrava ver' me la sua cera.
M'a sì mal punto mangiai d'una pera,
che po' m'ha dato tanto di tormento,
che que' che so 'n inferno per un cento
hanno men mal di me 'n ogni manera.
Così m'avess'ella fatt'affogone
o mi si fosse ne la gola posta;
ch'i' non avesse gollato 'l boccone!
Ché non sare' a così mala posta –
avvegna certo ch'egli è gran ragione
che, chi si nuoce su, pur a lu' costa.

XLVI

There was a period when Becchina's air
Became so gracious I was quite contented;
No better prospects could have been presented,
So sweet to me her countenance and fair;
But in an evil hour I plucked a pear,*
Of which full soon I bitterly repented:
Not souls a hundred years in hell tormented
Have any inkling what my sufferings were.
I wish I had been seized by suffocation
And choked before a morsel of that fruit
Went down my throat upon that luckless day!
I wouldn't be in this sad situation;
For it's a law not many will dispute:
That when you sin, then you're the one who'll pay.

XLVII

"Becchin'amor!" – "Che vuo', falso tradito?"
"Che mi perdoni." – "Tu non ne se' degno."
"Merzé, per Deo!" – "Tu vien' molto gecchito."
"E verrò sempre." – "Che sarammi pegno?"
"La buona fé." – "Tu ne se' mal fornito."
"No inver' di te." – "Non calmar, ch'i' ne vegno."
"In che fallai?" – "Tu sa' ch'i' l'abbo udito."
"Dimmel', amor." – "Va', che ti vegn'un segno!"
"Vuo' pur ch'i' muoia?" – "Anzi mi par mill'anni."
"Tu non di' ben." – "Tu m'insegnerai."
"Ed i' morrò." – "Omè che tu m'inganni!"
"Die tel perdoni." – "E che, non te ne vai?"
"Or potess'io!" – "Tègnoti per li panni?"
"Tu tieni 'l cuore." – "E terrò co' tuoi' guai."

XLVII

"Becchina dear!" – "What do you want from me?"
"Pardon." – "You don't deserve to hear the name."
"For Heaven's sake, mercy!" – "You've become quite tame."
"I'll be so always." – "Where's your guarantee?"
"In my good faith." – "You've none that I can see."
"I have for you." – "Don't try and calm me down."
"What's my offence?" – "The tale's all over town."
"What tale, my love?" – "Lord, scar him! Hear my plea!"
"You want me dead?" – "Can't wait to see it done."
"Now, that's no way to talk." – "You teach me how."
"Then I must die." – "If only that were true!"
"May God forgive you." – "What, you haven't gone?"
"Ah, if I could!" – "Who holds your coat-tail now?"
"You hold my heart." – "Yes, all the worse for you!"

XLVIII

Da Giuda in fuor, neuno sciagurato
fu né sarà di chi a cento mili'anni
ch'a mille miglia m'appressisi a' panni;
e sol m'avvien per ch'i' so 'nnamorato
di tal c'ha tutto 'l cuor avviluppato
di tradimento, di frode e d'inganni:
ed e' non fu sì leal san Giovanni
a Geso Cristo com'i' le son stato!
Ma la falsa natura femminile
sempre fu e sarà sanza ragione,
per ciò cad Eva diè lor quello stile.
Ond'i' son fermo 'n questa oppinïone:
di sempre starle gecchit' ed umìle,
poi ch'ell'ha scusa di sì gran cagione.

XLVIII

Not since the days of Judas has there been,
Nor will be for a hundred thousand years,
A single soul whose sorrows are so keen
As mine, because the one I love appears
To have a woman's heart wrapped in a hide
Of broken faith and trickery and fraud,
Though I was loyal to her on my side
As good Saint John was once to Christ our Lord.
But the false character of womankind
Has ever been and will be without reason
Because they got that style from Mother Eve.
And that is why I will not change my mind,
But still be humble to her and believe
She has a great excuse for all her treason.

XLIX

Qualunque giorno non veggio 'l mi' amore,
la notte come serpe mi travollo
e sì mi giro che paio un bigollo,
tanta è la pena che sente 'l meo core.
Parmi la notte ben cento mili'ore,
dicendo: "Dio, sarà ma' dì, vedrollo?" –
e tanto piango che tutto m'immollo,
ch'alcuna cosa m'alleggia 'l dolore.
Ed i' ne son da lei così cangiato
che 'n una ched e' giungo 'n sua contrada
sì mi fa dir ch'i' vi son troppo stato
e ched i' voli, sì tosto men vada,
però ch'ell'ha 'l su' amor a tal donato
che per un mille più di me li aggrada.

XLIX

At night, when all the day I failed to see
The one I love, I writhe like any snake;
Just like a spinning-top, it seems to me,
I'm turned around by Love and kept awake.
The night could be two hundred thousand hours,
So that I groan: "Will morning never break?"
I weep my pillow wet in bitter showers,
And nothing can relieve the endless ache.
So changed is life on her account today
That even when I walk along her street,
Someone complains I'm loitering by the way,
And hints that I should beat a quick retreat;
Because my lady's found another minion,
A thousand times more fit in her opinion.

L

Lassa la vita mia dolente molto,
ch'i' nacqui, credo, sol per mal avere,
poi che 'l me' grande diletto m'è tolto
in guisa tal, per giamma' non ravere:
ch'i' seminai ed un altr'ha ricolto;
s'i' me ne vogli'atar, non n'ho 'l potere,
per che la morte m'è già su nel volto:
così foss'ell'al cor a mi' piacere!
Neun'altra speranz' ho che di morte,
e mort'è quella che mi può guerire,
tant'è la pena mïa dura e forte.
Così sarebb'a me vita 'l morire,
puo' che cota' novelle mi fuor pòrte,
com'a pregion sentenziato 'l fuggire.

L

This wretched life has wearied me so sore,
It seems that I was born for this distress;
For I've been robbed of a great happiness
That nothing in this world can now restore.
Another reaps where I have sown before;
In vain I struggle, I am sheer outworn:
Death comes and settles in my face forlorn;
That he might still my heart would please me more.
There's now no hope but Death that I can see,
Sole doctor who can cure me, since so great
My sickness is, so pitiable my fate.
I welcome Death that would be life to me:
The news of it would leave me in the state
Of a condemned man who escapes scot-free.

LI

Maladetta sie l'or' e 'l punt'e 'l giorno
e la semana e 'l mese e tutto l'anno
che la mia donna mi fece uno 'nganno,
il qual m'ha tolt'al cuor ogni soggiorno,
ed hal sì 'nvolto tutto 'ntorno intorno
d'empiezza, d'ira, di noia e d'affanno
che, per mio bene e per mi' minor danno,
vorre'lo 'nnanzi 'n un ardente forno.
Però che megli'è mal che mal e peggio,
avvegna l'un e l'altro buon non sia,
per avere men pena i' 'l male chieggio.
E questo dico per l'anima mia:
ché, se non fosse ch'i' temo la peggio,
i' medesimo già morto m'avrìa.

LI

Cursed be the very moment, hour and day
Week, month and year, in which, with guile unmatched,
My lady played me false, and fiercely snatched
At one fell swoop my peace of mind away;
Then wrapped my heart about, to my dismay,
With malice, wrath, disgust, and such distress
That now I think that I would suffer less
If in a furnace it were burned away.
Yet since the bad is better than the worse
(Though neither of them suits me very well),
I'll bear as best I can with present woe.
Upon my soul's account I write this verse;
For were I not so terrified of hell,
I should have killed myself some time ago.

LII

I' m'ho onde dar pace e debbo e voglio,
sed i' ho punto di ragion con meco;
po' ch'e' con la mia donna stat'è seco,
so che giammai non debbo sentir doglio.
Di gioia mi vesto, di noia mi spoglio,
e ciò, ben ch'è 'n l'amor, a me' l'arreco;
ben posso dire: "*Ave, Dominus teco*",
poi mi guardò di venir a lo scoglio;
del quale i' era sì forte temente
ch'a tutte l'ore ch'i' a ciò pensava
sì dardellava tutto a dente a dente,
e non ch'altrui, ma me stess'odïava.
Or moglie vo' com'i' odio 'l gaudente –
ma innanzi tratto ben so com'andava.

LII

At last I should have peace; I'll have it too,
If I've a grain of gumption left in store:
Now that he's had her, I can bid Adieu,
And there's no reason I should suffer more.
I'll put off grief, and joy I'll don anew;
Love's cure is sharp, but that I'll not deplore.
Ave, Dominus tecum!* Thanks to you,
My bark has now escaped the fatal shore.
The thought of shipwreck filled me with such dread
I trembled, and my anguish was so great
That all my teeth were chattering. In that state
I loathed no others, but myself instead.
Now, as I hate the Friar, I need a wife,
Knowing the way things went in my old life.

LIII

Io vorre' 'nanzi 'n grazia ritornare
di quella donna che m'ha 'n signoria
com'io fu' già, ch'i' non vorrei trovare
un fiume che menass'òr tuttavia:
ché non è cuor che potessi pensare
quanta allegrezza sarebbe la mia;
ed or sanza 'l su' amor mi pare stare
come colu' ch'a la morte s'avvia.
Avvegna ched e' m'è bene 'nvestito,
ché io medesmo la colpa me n'abbo,
po' ch'i' non fo vendetta del marito,
che le fa peggio ch'a me non fa 'l babbo:
ed io, dolente! son sì 'mpoverito
ch'udendol dir sì me ne rido e gabbo.

LIII

Now I would rather be the favoured lover
Of that fair lady whom I still adore,
As once I was, than I would fain discover
A stream that washed up gold for evermore:
There's not a man who could divine the measure
Of half the gladness that would be my store;
While, barred from love, I'm lost to every pleasure,
And feel like one who's lying at death's door.
And yet, it seems that rightly I inherit
This plight, since I from guilt am hardly free;
For I don't give her husband what he merits,
Who treats her even worse than Dad treats me.
But sorrow's worn my courage down so thin,
That when I hear men say so, I just grin.

LIV

"Becchina, poi che tu mi fosti tolta,
che già è du' anni e paionmi ben cento,
sempre l'anima mia è stata 'nvolta
d'angoscia, di dolor e di tormento."
"Cecco, la pena tua credo sia molta,
ma più sarebbe per lo mi' talento;
s'i' dico tort'o dritto, pur ascolta:
perché non hai chi mi ti tolse spento?"
"Becchina, 'l core non mi può soffrire,
po' che per tua cagion ebbe la gioia,
a neun modo, di farlo morire."
"Cecco, s'una città come fu Troia
oggima' mi donassi, a lo ver dire,
non la vorre' per cavarti di noia."

LIV

"Becchina, since your love was robbed from me
Two years ago (a hundred years they seem),
My troubled soul has never ceased to be
Wrapped round about with agonies supreme."
"Cecco, I know your pains are quite severe,
Though not as great as I might well contrive;
Whether I'm talking sense or not, just hear:
Why is the man who robbed you still alive?"
"Becchina, since you gave it so much joy,
My heart is changed and never could consent,
On any terms, to make your husband die."
"Cecco, if you possessed a town like Troy,
I'd turn it down rather than I'd comply
With the one thing that cures your discontent."

LV

Ogn'altra carne m'è 'n odio venuta
e solamente d'un becco m'è 'n grado,
e d'essa m'è la voglia sì cresciuta
che, s'i' non n'ho, che Di' ne campi! arrado.
Quella cu' è mi dice ch'è venduta,
e ch'i' son folle, ch'i' averne bado;
ché, s'i' le dessi un marco d'òr trebuta,
non ne potre' avere quant'un dado.
Ed i', com'uomo cu' la fitta tocca,
ché so che voglion dir quelle parole,
sì do ad altre novelle di bocca.
E Die sa come 'l cor forte mi dole,
per ch'i' non ho de' fiorin a ribocca
per poter far e dir ciò ch'ella vuole.

LV

There is no kind of meat that I would touch
Except a *becco** (as we call the goat),
And this, indeed, I hunger for so much
That when it lacks foul curses choke my throat.
Goddam! I hear that all the stock is sold
And that I'm mad to want such dainty fare;
And, what is more, even a mark of gold
Would hardly buy a morsel for my share.
Then, like a man gripped with a sudden pain,
Because I guess what all these words convey,
I start to sing in quite a different key.
God knows my heart is sore and aches in vain;
I've not a florin I can spare today
To say or do all that she wants of me.

LVI

Credenza sia – ma sì 'l sappia chi vuole –
ch'i' ho donat' una cos'a Becchina
che, s'io non l'ho staser'o domattina,
daroll'a diveder che me ne duole;
ché non è or quel tempo ch'esser suole,
merzé de l'alta potenza divina,
che m'ha cavato di cuor quella spina
che punge com'uliscono le viuole.
La quale spina Amor noma la gente –
ma chi lel pose non lesse la chiosa
e, s'e' la lesse, sì seppe nïente:
ch'i' dico ch'ell'è spina sanza rosa;
ch'om ch'ella punge dir può lealmente
che la mie costïon non si è dubbiosa.

LVI

It is a secret any man may know,
There's something I have let Becchina borrow;
Yet if she doesn't give it back tomorrow
She'll see how lightly I can let it go.
For times have changed, and for the change I owe
My thanks to God who plucked from out my heart
The thorn embedded there whose pungent smart
Pervaded all, like violets when they blow.
The thorn is Love; so called, one must suppose,
By men of most restricted erudition,
For what they say leaves something crucial out.
I tell you Love's a thorn without a rose,
And all those pricked allow this definition;
I've proved the fact beyond the slightest doubt.

LVII

S'i' mi ricordo ben, i' fu' d'amore
il più 'nnamorat'om che fosse mai,
ché s'io stava l'anno pur due ore
fuor di mia terra, traea mille guai;
e quella ch'era mia donna e signore
isperanza di ben mi dava assai,
e puo' infine, per pietà di cuore,
di lei mi donò ciò ch'io disïai.
Or che m'avvenne per la mie sventura?
Che, partendo da lei, in un momento
ella disamorò ed io ancora.
Dunqua, quanto mi fuora in piacimento
che fosse a far ciò ched i' feci allora,
sì mi truovo senz'amor l'un del cento.

LVII

If I remember well, I must have been
The fondest lover that has e'er adored;
Two hours' absence in a year was seen
As some immense disaster I deplored:
While she that was my lady and my lord
Teased me with hopes of ultimate fruition,
Until at last she gave what I implored
Out of sheer pity for my sad condition.
But what has happened now, to my dismay?
Leaving her for a moment was enough
To see both passions, mine and hers, abating.
So, though I wish I could repeat today
Old pleasures, still I would be better off
Than I am now if she had kept me waiting.

LVIII

Sed i' fossi costretto di pigliare
tra d'essere 'n inferno o 'nnamorato,
sed i' non mi pugnasse a consigliare,
unque Dio non perdoni 'l mi' peccato;
per ch'i' non posso creder né pensare
che sia neun dolore addolorato
maggio ch'i' ho sofferto per amare
quella che m'ha d'Amor sì spaurato.
Ma, s'io prendessi di rinnamorarmi,
in questo nodo mi v'accordarei:
ch'Amor dovesse 'n prima sicurarmi
di quella che m'ha mort'anni fa sei,
che non dovesse su' pregio tornarmi –
se non, lo 'nfern'a gran boce cherrei.

LVIII

Now if, let us suppose, I should be driven
To opt for Love or Hell, and I thus placed
Made choice perhaps with an unseemly haste,
I trust to God my choice would be forgiven.
I can't believe, although my mind has striven
To do so, that some other pains could mount
Higher than those I bear on Love's account,
By which today my heart is racked and riven.
Yet if I chose to love again, I know
I would demand at least this guarantee:
The girl who caused my death six years ago
Should never use her gifts to torture me.
From Love this solemn promise I'd compel:
If not, be sure you'd hear me howl for Hell.

LIX

Qual uomo vuol purgar le sue peccata,
sed e' n'avesse quanti n'ebbe Giuda,
faccia pur sì ched egli abbia una druda,
la qual sia d'un altr'uomo 'nnamorata.
Se non gli secca 'l cuor e la curata,
mostrandosi di lui cotanto cruda,
ch'e' mi sia dato d'una spada gnuda,
che pur allotta allotta sia arrotata.
Potrebbono già dir: "Tu come 'l sai?"
I' li rispondarei che l'ho provato,
ché per la mia sciagura una n'amai
la qual ha il cor d'un altro sì piagato
che mi facea trar più rata e più guai
che non fa l'uom quand'è verrucolato.

LIX

Now he who'd purge himself of all his sins,
Though numberless like Judas's, should plan
To take a concubine, when he begins,
Who is enamoured of some other man;
And if his heart and bowels remain unchastened
By all the torture of her fierce intent,
Then let the period of my years be hastened
By sword well sharpened up for that event.
Someone might want to ask: "How can you know?"
My answer is, I've proved the matter true:
I loved a woman once, some time ago,
Heart-wounded by another; and I too
Found myself screaming, tortured no less fully
Than some poor wretch being strung up by the pulley.

LX

Io combattei con Amor ed hol morto,
e ch'i' ho tanto pugnato mi pento;
però ch'i' ebbi 'l dritto ed elli 'l torto,
convenne pur che rimanesse vénto:
ch'e' mi promise conduciarm'a porto
e puo' mi volse vele con un vento,
che se non fosse ch'io ne fui accorto,
rotto m'avrebbe 'n mar a tradimento.
Ma 'nanzi ch'i' vencesse la battaglia,
già non mi seppi da lui sì schermire
ch'e' non mi dess'un colpo a la sgaraglia
che m'ebbe presso che fatto morire;
ma pur infine non vals'una paglia,
ch'i' ne campai e lu' feci perire.

LX

I fought with Love, whom I at last have slain,
And only grieve I took so long to fight;
Yet still, since he was wrong and I was right,
That he should lose the war was pretty plain.
He swore he'd guide me into port again,
Then with a squall he turned my sails about:
Had I been unprepared, the sea, no doubt
Would treacherously have split my bark in twain.
Before our swords were crossed, I did not know
How to defend myself from one so dread;
I feared some master-thrust or swashing blow
Would end my days and cut the vital thread;
But now I see how feeble was my foe,
For I'm alive, and Love is surely dead.

LXI

Io sent'o sentirò ma' quel, d'Amore,
che sente que' che non fu anche nato;
cert'i non so s'i' me ne so' 'ngannato,
ché me ne par aver tratto 'l migliore;
ch'assa' val me' libertà che segnore,
e riposar che viver tribulato:
ché tutto 'l tempo ch'i' fu' 'nnamorato,
non seppi che foss'altro che dolore.
Or viv'e cant'en allegrezza e riso,
e non so che si sia malinconia,
tanto m'allegra da lu' star diviso.
E qual om vòl tener la dritta via
d'aver en questo mondo 'l paradiso,
mortal nemico d'Amor sempre sia.

LXI

I feel no more the sting of Love today
Than does the babe unborn within its breast;
If I deceive myself I cannot say,
But still I hope all's settled for the best.
Freedom's worth more than life beneath his sway,
Repose is better than to live distressed,
For all the time Love held me as his prey
I had no pause from pain, nor any rest.
And now I live and laugh and sing for joy,
And know no more the meaning of annoy,
Because I am no longer passion's thrall.
To him that seeks an earthly paradise,
Before he starts I offer this advice:
He'll need to be Love's foe for good and all.

LXII

I' sono innamorato, ma non tanto
che non men passi ben leggeramente;
di ciò mi lodo e tègnomi valente,
ch'a l'Amor non so' dato tutto quanto.
E' basta ben se per lui gioco e canto
e amo e serverìa chi gli è servente:
ogni soperchio val quanto nïente,
e ciò non regna en me, ben mi do vanto.
Però non pensi donna che sia nata
che l'ami ligio com'i' veggio molti,
sia quanto voglia bella e delicata,
ché troppo amare fa gli òmini stolti –
però non vo' tener cotal usata
che cangia 'l cor e divisa gli volti.

LXII

Yes, I'm in love, but not so much that I
Can't do without it when I will discreetly;
And so I vaunt my courage loud and high,
For Love has failed to capture me completely.
It is enough I play to him and sing,
And serve and cherish those who call him Master:
Excess has never brought man anything,
It can't rule me or bring me to disaster.
Let never a woman born imagine then
That I'm her slave like many that I see,
For all her lovely airs and subtle graces;
It's too much loving that makes fools of men:
No way of life commends itself to me
That saddens hearts and alters happy faces.

LXIII

E' non ha tante gocciole nel mare
ched i' non abbia più pentute 'n core:
ch'i' concedetti di prender la fiore
ch'ella degnò di volermi donare –
quella che Dio non ebb'altro che fare,
quando la fece, tant'ha 'n sé valore.
E chi dicesse "Te ne 'nganna Amore"
vad'a vederla e a udirla parlare.
E abbia cuor di pietra baldamente
s'e' non ritorna di lei 'nnamorato,
sì dica: "Cecco, 'l tu' sonetto mente" –
ch'ell'ha 'l su' viso tanto dilicato
ch'al mondo non ha niun così vivente.
Così non fosse quel vis'ancor nato!

LXIII

More than the droplets that are in the sea
Are the regrets with which my heart is full,
Because, too deeply charmed, I stooped to cull
The flower that my lady offered me.
God must have had no other work in hand
When he framed so much worth in heaven above;
And if you think that I'm deceived by Love,
Go see her, hear her speak: you'll understand.
Your heart must be far harder than a stone
If you're not deep in love when you return;
I dare you then to say this sonnet lies.
Her features are so fine and sweet, you'll own
There's nothing quite like her beneath the skies.
Would God that lovely face were not yet born!

LXIV

Or se ne vada chi è innamorato,
ch'e' può dir che la madre il maladisse
gran tempo innanzi ch'ella il partorisse,
o che dal padre fosse ingenerato.
Per me lo dico, ch'i' l'aggio provato
el mio cor tristo che 'n amor si misse
en sì mal tempo che già mai non visse
un'ora solamente riposato!
E sì m'è avviso ch'or ne vien la bella:
ché tutto il tempo della vita mia
non ebbe né avrò sì ria novella.
E credo che 'ntervien, chi vuol chi sia,
che se muor la sua donna e sia pulcella,
ch'a la sua vita avrà malinconia.

LXIV

To any man in love I this declare:
Your mother cursed you to a heavy doom
Even before she forced you from the womb,
Even before your father put you there.
I'm judging by myself in what I say,
For since my heart, upon an evil hour,
Became a humble slave to passion's power,
My rest has gone and grief has come to stay.
And now here comes the bitterest blow of all:
There's never been a single greater scourge in
Any man's life, nor will there be tomorrow.
I've not a doubt, whatever may befall,
That if your lady dies while still a virgin,
Your days are doomed to everlasting sorrow.

LXV

Tutto quest'anno ch'è, mi son frustato
di tutti i vizi che solìa avere:
non m'è rimasto se non quel di bere,
del qual me n'abbi Iddio per escusato,
ché la mattina, quando son levato,
el corpo pien di sal mi par avere –
adunque di': chi si porìa tenere
di non bagnarsi la lingua e 'l palato?
E non vorrìa se non greco e vernaccia,
ché mi fa maggior noia il vin latino
che la mia donna, quand'ella mi caccia.
Deh, ben abbi chi prima pose 'l vino,
che tutto 'l dì mi fa star in bonaccia –
i' non ne fo però un mal latino.

LXV

Throughout this year I duly have restrained
Every habitual vice excepting drink,
From which, it's true, I have not quite refrained,
But God's forgiven me for that, I think.
Each morn it seems to me when I arise,
As if my body were filled up with salt;
Then say who would forbear, however wise,
From washing out his mouth? It's not my fault.
I only want Vernaccia* or Greek wine,
I loathe your common house wine, which is sour,
As sour as my wife, and so I hate it.
God bless the man who first improved the vine,
To which I owe full many a happy hour;
I'll never say a word to denigrate it.

LXVI

In questo mondo, chi non ha moneta
per forza è necessario che si ficchi
un spiedo per lo corpo o che si 'mpicchi,
se tanto è savio che curi le peta.
Ma chi lo staio ha pieno o la galleta,
avvegna ch'i' nol posso dir per micchi,
di ciò trabocca, nïente men picchi
per su' argento, che fa l'uom poeta.
Ancor ci ha altro, che detto non abbo:
che l'ammalato sì fa san venire,
terre tenere, a quel ch'io vi dirabbo;
e 'l mercennaro sì fa 'ngentilire,
buono, saccente e cortese: s'io gabbo,
sì prego Dio che mi faccia morire.

LXVI

In this world anyone devoid of pelf
Should try impalement on a spit, or find
A friendly beam on which to hang himself,
Or test his wit by farting in the wind.
While he whose measure's full, and something more,
(Mine never has been yet) is still inclined
To stoop to any trick to swell his store
Of gold which gives a man a poet's mind.
There's something I've left out, I'll say it then:
Broad lands and fertile acres are the best
Cure for disease and surely stop the rot;
They change vile rascals into gentlemen,
Most good and wise and courteous. If I jest,
May God almighty strike me on the spot.

LXVII

Cosi è l'uomo che non ha denari
com'è l'uccel quand'è vivo pelato:
li uomin di salutarlo li son cari –
com'un malatto sel veggion da lato.
E' dolci pomi li paion amari,
e ciò ch'elli od'e vede li è disgrato;
per lu' ritornan li cortes'avari:
or quest'è 'l secol del pover malfato.
Un rimedi'ha per lu' in questo mondo:
ched e' s'affogh'anz'oggi che domane,
ché fa per lu' la mort'e non la vita.
Ma que' c'ha la sua borsa ben fornita,
ogn'uom li dice: "Tu se' me' che 'l pane,"
e ciò che vòl come mazza va a tondo.

LXVII

The man who has no more the means to pay
Is like a live bird plucked of every feather;
His friends forget to greet him – that's when they
Don't shun him like infection altogether.
And what was sweet is bitter fruit today,
While every sight and sound makes his soul sicken;
Kindness itself grows hard and turns away,
Thus fares the wretch whom poverty has stricken.
The world's one remedy for all this sorrow
Is: "Go and drown yourself, you're better dead;
Do it today, don't leave it for tomorrow."
But he whose stuffed purse shows him to be rich
Is praised by all as better than fresh bread,
And what he plans succeeds without a hitch.

LXVIII

Se l'omo avesse 'n sé conoscimento,
in tutto lasserebbe Amore stare,
se non avesse di quel fornimento
che sì bisogna a quei che vòl amare:
ciò è di fiorin molti abbondamento,
e ricche gioie per poter donare
a quella donna ch'elli ha en piacimento,
sì ch'alcun don da lei possa acquistare
e possa star gioioso tra la gente,
e non sia per alcun mostrato a dito,
né fatto di lui beffe spessamente.
Chéd e' si vede l'om ch'è arricchito,
che, per amar basso o vòi altamente,
quello ch'e' fa sì è sempre gradito.

LXVIII

A man who truly knows what's for the best
Will surely leave the god of Love alone,
Unless indeed he happens to be blessed
With everything a lover ought to own;
Such as a pile of florins in his pocket
Or precious jewellery he can transfer
To his sweet lady who delights to stock it,
And that's how he buys any gift from her,
And swaggers happily among the crowd;
No one will ever point him out in shame
Or even make a joke that might offend.
A man whose purse is properly endowed
Can love both high and low, it's all the same,
Do what he likes and never lack a friend.

LXIX

Or udite, signor, s'i' ho ragione
ben di dovermi impiccar per la gola:
poi che la povertà mi ten a scola,
madonna m'ha più a vile ch'un muscione;
ché l'ho sincerata a molte stagione,
e quando accompagnata e quando sola:
e s'eo li dico pur una parola,
mi fa vergogna più ch'a un ladrone.
E tutto mel fa far la povertate!
Quand'ei denar, non me solea venire,
poi ch'avea en borsa la gran degnitate:
ciò è 'l fiorin, che fammi risbaldire,
ed a mia donna mi tol la viltate,
quando non dice che mi vòl servire.

LXIX

Now listen, sir, if my opinion's right,
I should be hanged (there's little doubt of that):
Since poverty has brought me to this plight,
My lady thinks I'm worthless as a gnat.
I've proved my love, both in and out of season;
Alone or not, I served her just the same;
Now, if I try a word or two of reason,
I'm treated like robber, to my shame.
All this because I'm poor! When I had gold,
Nothing like that could happen to me here,
For my fat purse was dignity enough:
A florin's all it took to make me bold,
I boarded her without the slightest fear
Even when she played coy and put me off.

LXX

Un danaio, non che far cottardita,
avessi sol, tristo! ne la mia borsa:
ch'e' mi conven far di quelle de l'orsa,
che per la fame si lecca le dita;
e non avrò già tanto a la mia vita –
o lasso me! – ch'io ne faccia gran torsa,
da poi che la ventura m'è sì scorsa
ch'andando per la via ogn'uom m'addita.
Or dunque, che vita sarà la mia
se non di comperare una ritorta
e d'appiccarmi sopresso una via,
e far tutte le morti ad una volta,
ch'i' ne fo ben cento milia la dia?
Ma solo il gran peccato mi sconforta.

LXX

If only I had one last coin to spare,
I'd let you have it for your gown, alright!
Instead I'm forced to imitate the bear,
Who licks his paws to blunt his appetite.
My future isn't likely to be bright
With shining coins and money bags replete:
Since Fortune treated me with so much spite,
Men point their fingers at me in the street.
What other way is there for me to mend
This wretched life, except to go and choose
A rope to help me to a fitting end,
Contracting all my sorrows to a noose?
A thousand deaths I have already died,
But still I fear the sin of suicide.

LXXI

Di tutte cose mi sento fornito,
se non d'alquante ch'i' non metto cura,
come di calzamento e d'armadura;
di ben vestire i' son tutto pulito,
e co' danari son sì mal nodrito,
più ch'i' del diavol, di me han paura;
altri diletti, per mala ventura,
più ne son fuor che gennaio del fiorito.
Ma sapete di che i' ho abbondanza?
Di ma' desnar con le cene peggiori,
e male letta, per compier la danza.
Gli altri disagi non conto, signori,
ché troppo sarebbe lunga la stanza:
questi so' nulla, appo gli altri maggiori.

LXXI

At least what I possess is comprehensive,
Save for some things I make no fuss about:
For instance, shoes and armour that's defensive;
While of good clothing I am quite cleared out.
My purse is lean (though life's not less expensive)
So that I'm shunned like him of evil powers;
And as for other joys, they're so extensive
I bloom with them like January with flowers.
Yet would you know with what I'm well provided?
With meagre dinners, suppers even worse,
And beds that serve only for sleep's prevention.
And here I'll stop lest I should be derided
For going on beyond the bounds of verse:
Such ills are nothing to those I could mention.

LXXII

La povertà m'ha sì disamorato
che, s'i' scontro mie donna entro la via,
a pena la conosco, 'n fede mia,
e 'l nome ho già quasi dimenticato.
Da l'altra parte m'ha 'l cuor sì agghiacciato
che, se mi fosse fatta villania
dal più agevol villanel che sia,
di me non avrebb'altro che 'l peccato.
Ancor m'ha fatto vie più sozzo gioco:
ché tal solev'usar meco a diletto
che, s'i' 'l pur miro, sì li paio un foco.
Ond'i' vo' questo motto aver per detto:
che s'uom dovesse stare con un cuoco,
sì 'l dovrìa far per non vivarci bretto.

LXXII

Now poverty has cooled my love at last;
So if, while walking in the street, I met
My lady, I'm convinced that I'd forget
Her name, and hardly know her as she passed.
My heart's so frozen by the plight I'm in
That if I were insulted, I believe,
By the most vile of cowards, he'd receive
Nothing from me except the name of sin.
But here's the nastiest joke of penury,
That one whose friendship always brought me joy
Now shrinks away as from a conflagration.
This is the only proverb fit for me:
If it's your fate to be a kitchen-boy,
Then turn the spit, it's better than starvation.

LXXIII

I' son sì magro che quasi traluco –
de la persona no, ma de l'avere;
ed abbo tanto più a dar che avere,
che m'è rimaso vie men d'un fistuco.
Ed èmmi sì turato ogni mi' buco
ch'i' ho po' che dar e vie men che tenere:
ben m'è ancora rimas'un podere
che frutta l'anno il valer d'un sambuco!
Ma non ci ha forza, ch'i so 'nnamorato –
ché s'i' avesse più òr che non sale,
per me sarìa 'n poco temp'assommato.
Or mi paresse almeno pur far male!
Ma com più struggo, più son avvïato
di voler far di nuovo capitale.

LXXIII

So lean that I'm transparent, that's my style –
In person no, in goods and chattels yes.
My debts exceed my funds to such excess
That scarce a straw remains of all my pile.
No source of cash that's not bunged up, I fear;
I've nothing left to give and less to hold,
Though there's a farm that hasn't yet been sold
And brings me less than sixpence in a year.
Yet nothing stops me being in love, I vow
That if I had more gold than there is salt,
I'd spend the lot of it without delay.
If I could only stop the rot right now!
But no, the more I spend the more my fault
Is looking for fresh funds to throw away.

LXXIV

A chi nol sa non lasci Dio provare
ch'è, del poco, volere fare assai;
e se tu mi domandi: "Come 'l sai?" –
per che 'n danar mi veggio menomare
e ne le spese crescere e montare,
sed io onore ci voglio giammai.
Di' dunque, smemorato: or che farai?
Se fossi savio, andrestit'a 'mpiccare.
Non aspettar che tu abbi assommato,
ché troppo ti fia peggio che 'l morire:
ed io lo so, che vegno dal mercato;
ché 'lmen tre volte il dì 'l veggio avvenire,
m'assal povèrta anzi ch'i' sia corcato:
ciò è al levare, al mangiare, al dormire.

LXXIV

To one that does not know let God not tell
How ends that do not touch are made to meet;
And if you ask how I know that so well,
The answer's this: my purse is incomplete;
For still expenses mount, but can't compete
In size with the great debt that honour owes.
So what, my giddy friend, would you propose?
To hang yourself, I think, would be discreet.
O never wait till all be spent, like some,
For worse than now will be your ruin then,
As I, who quit the market, can attest.
At least three times a day I see him come,
Grim shade of Poverty, and that is when
I wake, sit down to eat, and go to rest.

LXXV

In una ch'e' danar mi danno meno,
anco che pochi me n'entrano 'n mano,
son come vin ch'è du' part'acqua, leno,
e son più vil che non fu pro' Tristano;
e 'nfra le genti vo col capo 'n seno,
più vergognoso ch'un can foretano;
e per averne dì e notte peno,
ciò è in modo che non sia villano.
E sì avvien talor, per avventura,
ch'alquanti me ne vegnon uncicati,
de' quali fo sì gran manicatura
ch'anz'i' gli abbia son quasi logorati:
ché non mi piace 'l prestar ad usura
a mo' de' preti e de' ghiotton frati.

LXXV

As my supply of cash keeps getting shorter
(Not that I ever had that much to hold),
I feel as weak as wine that's two thirds water
And more a coward than Tristan was bold.
More shamefaced than a skulking homeless hound,
I walk the world with head hung down, and go
To seek where some rare florins might be found
In any way that isn't vile and low.
And if, from time to time, I hook a few
When lucky chance unlocks the precious store,
I spend until they're swallowed up anew,
And I'm the beggar that I was before:
For I won't lend on interest like those liars,
The greedy priesthood and the glutton friars.

LXXVI

Quando non ho denar, ogn'om mi schiva
e non par che mi cognosca om del mondo;
a dir che canti o che soni la piva,
niente mi vale senza lo ritondo;
ch'e' non rimagna spesso su la riva
neun mi leva, per lo grave pondo;
allor mi stringo com'in nave stiva,
ed in la cera tutto mi nascondo.
E buffo forte e tro di gran sospiri,
e faccio di quelle di Mongibello,
sì com'el lupo che non trova carne.
Tutto che non mi paia bon né bello,
quel mi governa dove che mi giri:
non ho altro ridotto ove m'aitarne.

LXXVI

When I've no money left men turn away,
I'm someone they don't want to know or see;
Playing the pipes or singing through the day
Won't help a wretch without a groat like me.
When I am lying stranded on the shore
Nobody tries to lift my heavy weight;
Like some tight vessel's hold with precious store,
I lock myself away to hide my state.
I pant, I fume, I heave enormous sighs,
Outbellow Etna, howling with the greed
Of some stray wolf who's looking out for meat.
All that's most foul and ugly to my eyes
Rules me wherever I may roam: my need
Can find no other succour or retreat.

LXXVII

Ogne mie 'ntendimento mi ricide
el non aver denari 'n cavaglione,
e vivo matto com'uom ch'è 'n pregione,
pregando Morte: "Per Di', or m'uccide!"
E quand'i' n'ho, tutto 'l mondo mi ride,
ed ogni cosa mi va a ragione,
e son vie più ardito ch'un leone:
ben tegno folle chi da sé i divide.
Ma s'i' veggio mai 'l dì ch'i' ne raggiunga,
ben lo terrò più savio che Merlino,
a ch'i dena' mi trarrà de la punga.
E di gavazze parrò fiorentino,
e parrammi mill'anni ch'i riponga,
po' che m'è mess'a trentun l'aquilino.

LXXVII

See, all my plans and resolutions fail
Because I've got no florins in my breeches:
I'm quite as mad as any wretch in jail
When "Kill me now, for God's sake!" he beseeches.
When I am flush, men say to me "All hail!"
And everything is sweet to me as honey;
I feel as brave as lions on the trail,
Which teaches us to hold on to our money.
If someday cash should once again be mine,
I'll be as wise as Merlin, and resist
Before they prise a penny from my fist;
I'll spend as freely as a Florentine.*
However much I save won't seem enough
When I remember how I lost the stuff.

LXXVIII

In nessun modo mi poss'acconciare
ad aver voglia di far masserizia:
e non averìa 'l cor quella letizia,
che quando penso di volerla fare,
ch'i' non mi turbi com'om novo 'n mare;
e l'anim'entro 'l core mi s'affizia,
e di corrucci e d'ira ho tal dovizia
che ben ne posso vender e donare.
Assa' potrebb'om dar del cap'al muro,
ma se non ven de la propia natura,
nïente vale: 'n mia fede 'l vi giuro.
E non vi paia udire cosa oscura,
ché come 'l sarament'è stato puro,
così abb'io 'n mia donna ventura.

LXXVIII

I cannot bring myself in any way
To think about the need for some economy;
Joy leaves my heart and pleasure will not honour me,
The very thought's enough to spoil my day;
I'm sick like some new sailor on the sea,
My soul is plunged into such deep affliction;
Anger and irritation cause such friction,
Such bargaining was never meant for me.
Though you can butt your head against a wall,
You can't do what your nature won't allow;
It just won't work, I swear it on my life.
These words are not ambiguous at all:
They're quite as plain as any marriage vow,
And if they're not, then I can't trust my wife.

LXXIX

Per ogni oncia di carne che ho addosso,
e' ho ben cento libre di tristizia,
né non so che si sia a dir letizia:
così mia donna mi tene ad escosso.
Pare ch'ella mi franga d'osso in osso
quando mi dice: "Fa' ben massarizia,
e po' ti darò denari a divizia,"
anzi vorrei esser gittat'a un fosso.
E' non m'è viso che sia altro inferno
se non la massarizia maledetta –
e più mi spiace che 'l piover d'inverno.
Ma quale è vita santa e benedetta,
secondo i gran medici di Salerno?
S'tu vòi star san, fa' ciò che ti diletta.

LXXIX

For every ounce of flesh that I may carry,
I bear at least a hundred pounds of sadness,
Till I've become a stranger to all gladness,
So close I'm kept by her they made me marry.
She grinds my very bones with phrases which
Advise economy; here's one example:
"Take care and your allowance will be ample."
I'd rather have them throw me in a ditch!
There simmers no such terrible Inferno
As this cursed economical persistence;
It's worse than winter rain that falls and freezes.
What say the learnèd doctors of Salerno
About a holy and a blessed existence?
That man is healthy who does what he pleases.

LXXX

La stremità mi richer per figliuolo,
ed i' l'appello ben per madre mia;
e 'ngenerato fu' dal fitto duolo,
e la mia bàlia fu malinconia,
e le mie fasce si fur d'un lenzuolo
che volgarment'ha nome riccadìa;
da la cima del capo 'nfin al suolo,
cosa non regna 'n me che bona sia.
Po' quand'i' fu' cresciuto, mi fu dato
per mia ristorazion moglie che garre
da anzi dì 'nfin al ciel stellato;
e 'l su' garrir paion mille chitarre:
a cu' la moglie muor, ben è lavato
se la ripiglia, più che non è 'l Farre.

LXXX

I was brought forth by Misery distressed,
Though Mother is the term that I would rather;
Sorrow begot me, and I called him Father,
And Melancholy nursed me at her breast.
Fold after fold, the swaddling clothes that pressed
My baby limbs were pleated with annoy;
And so from head to foot the little boy
With nothing good was governed and was dressed.
When I was grown into a man they found
A wife to comfort me with voice that jars
The very heavens above, a jangling sound
Like the perpetual strumming of guitars.
Thus any man whose wife has died is reckoned
A hopeless fool if he should take a second.

LXXXI

Per sì gran somma ho 'mpegnate le risa
che io non so vedere come possa
prendere modo di far la rescossa:
per più l'ho 'n pegno che non monta Pisa.
Ed è sì forte la mia mente assisa
che prima mi lassarei franger l'ossa
che ad un sol ghigno io facesse mossa,
tanto son dagli spiriti 'n recisa.
L'altro giorno voler mi parve, 'n sogno,
un atto fare che rider valesse:
svegliàimi – certo ancor me ne vergogno.
E dico fra me stesso: "Dio volesse
ch'i' fusse 'n quello stato ch'i' mi pogno,
ch'uccidere farìa chiunca ridesse!"

LXXXI

I've mortgaged merriment for such a sum
That how I'll pay it off I just can't see;
The value of all Pisa wouldn't come
To the amount that now is asked of me.
Indeed, I'm so determined to be glum
They'd have to grind my bones before a grin
Defaced my facial muscles that are numb,
And that's the kind of broken state I'm in.
The other day, deep in a dream, I came
Close to an act that might have been some fun:
I woke (of course!) to a great sense of shame.
And so I mutter to myself: "I vow,
If God allowed, I would kill anyone
Who's reading this and laughing at me now."

LXXXII

I' ho sì poco di quel ch'i' vorrei
ch'i' non so ch'i' potesse menomare;
e sì mi poss'un cotal vanto dare
che del contraro par non trovarei;
ché s'i' andass'al mar, non credarei
gocciola d'acqua potervi trovare:
sì ch'i son oggimai 'n sul montare,
ché, s'i' volesse, scender non potrei.
Però malinconia non prenderaggio,
anzi m'allegrerò del mi' tormento
come fa del rie tempo l'om selvaggio.
Ma' che m'aiuta sol un argomento:
ch'i aggio udito dire ad un om saggio
che ven un dì che val per più di cento.

LXXXII

Of all I want so very little's mine
That I believe I couldn't have much less;
Show me the luckiest man on earth, I guess
His fortune can't compare with my decline;
If I set off towards the sea, I think
I'd find less water than they use baptising:
So that today I'm sure I must be rising;
There isn't any lower I could sink.
Yet I'll not yield to whimpering despair,
But welcome my disasters in the way
That savages rejoice in foulest weather.
For once I heard a learnèd man declare:
To every man at length will dawn a day
That's worth a hundred others put together.

LXXXIII

Egli è maggior miracol com'io vivo –
cento milia cotanto, al me' parere –
che non serìa veder un olivo
che non fosse innestato menar pere,
e che non serìa far bon un cattivo
sì agevolmente come si fa 'l bere:
per ch'ogni cosa 'l dà 'l mio cor è privo
così com'è l'om cieco del vedere.
Ma' che m'aiuta un poco di speranza,
ché ho 'l me' cor più umil ca la seta:
gia mille volte serìa sotterrato!
Ma qualunch'ora i' ho più malenanza,
allor aspetto de la mia pianeta
che in ben per lei mi serà cambiato.

LXXXIII

It is a greater marvel I'm alive
(Greater a thousand times, it seems to me)
Than that, in spite of nature, pears should thrive,
Without being grafted, on an olive tree;
Greater than that a rogue should be set right,
Reformed as simply as he drinks, let's say:
Because, as surely as the blind lose sight,
My heart is robbed of everything today.
But still some hope is left to cheer my road,
Although my heart's so humble; otherwise
I should have died a thousand times already.
Just when I seem to sink beneath my load,
I trust my planet's working in the skies
To change my luck, and then to keep it steady.

LXXXIV

Se Die m'aiuti, a le sante guagnele,
s'i' veggio 'l dì sia 'n Siena ribandito,
se dato mi fosse 'n l'occhio col dito
a soffrire mi parrà latt'e mèle.
E parrò un colombo senza fele,
tanto starò di bon core gecchito:
però ch'i' abbo tanto mal patito
che pietade n'avrebb'ogni crudele.
E tutto questo mal mi parrebb'oro,
sed i' avesse pur tanta speranza
quant'han color che stanno 'n purgatoro.
Ma elli è tanta la mie sciaguranza,
ch'ivi farabb'a quell'otta dimoro
che babb'ed i' saremo in accordanza.

LXXXIV

I swear by all the Gospels that if I
Were called back to Siena, then so sunny
I'd feel that, if they poked me in the eye,
It still would seem to me like milk and honey.
I'd coo like any dove, devoid of gall,
My heart disposed in such a humble fashion
That, reckoning up my wrongs, I think that all,
Even my bitterest foes, would feel compassion.
I'd welcome all my suffering like gold
If I had half the hope of souls that spend
In Purgatory their allotted span.
The worst is this: my prospects are on hold;
They won't let me return, as I intend,
Unless I first make peace with my Old Man.*

LXXXV

Babb'e Becchina, l'Amor e mie madre
m'hanno sì come tord'a siepe stretto;
prima vo' dir quel che mi fa mi' padre:
che ciascun dì da lu' son maladetto.
Becchina vuole cose sì leggiadre
che non le fornirebbe Malcommetto.
Amor mi fa 'nvaghir di sì gran ladre
che par che sien figliuole di Gaetto.*
Mie madr'è lassa per la non potenza,
sì ch'i' lo debb'aver per ricevuto,
da po' ch'i so la sua malavoglienza.
L'altrier passa' per vi'e dièll'un saluto,
per disaccar la sua mal'accoglienza;
sì disse: "Cecco, va', che sie fenduto!"

LXXXV

Dad, my Becchina, Love and then my mother
Have caught me like a throstle in a net;
I'll take my father before any other,
His daily curses haven't dried up yet.
The goodies my Becchina craves or snitches
Could not be conjured up by Mahomet;*
Love always leads me to some thieving bitches,
The daughters of a bandit chief, I bet.
Though Mother now has grown too tired to go
And do much harm, her hate's so undiminished
It's just as bad as if she hadn't failed.
I saw her in the street two days ago
And greeted her, hoping our quarrel finished;
She answered: "Go and get yourself impaled!"

LXXXVI

S'i' fosse foco, arderei 'l mondo;
s'i' fosse vento, lo tempesterei;
s'i' fosse acqua, i' l'annegherei;
s'i' fosse Dio, mandereil'en profondo;
s'i' fosse papa, sare' allor giocondo,
ché tutti cristïani imbrigherei;
s'i' fosse 'mperator, sa' che farei?
A tutti mozzarei lo capo a tondo.
S'i' fosse morte, andarei da mio padre;
s'i' fosse vita, fuggirei da lui:
similemente farìa da mi' madre.
S'i' fosse Cecco, com'i' sono e fui,
torrei le donne giovani e leggiadre,
e vecchie e laide lasserei altrui.

LXXXVI

If I were fire, I'd set the world alight;
If I were wind, I'd surely blow it down;
If I were water, you would see it drown;
If I were God, I'd plunge it out of sight:
If I were Pope, then my supreme delight
Would be in making Christian lives a hell;
If I were Emperor (how can you tell?),
I'd chop off heads all round, both day and night.
If I were Death, I'd pay my Dad a visit;
If I were Life, he'd get what he deserved,
Because I'd run away from him and Mother.
If I were Cecco (not unlikely, is it?),
I'd have the lively lovely girls reserved,
And leave the old and ugly hags for others.

LXXXVII

Tre cose solamente mi so' 'n grado,
le quali posso non ben men fornire:
ciò è la donna, la taverna e 'l dado –
queste mi fanno 'l cuor lieto sentire.
Ma sì me le conven usar di rado,
ché la mie borsa mi mett'al mentire;
e quando mi sovvien, tutto mi sbrado,
ch'i' perdo per moneta 'l mie disire.
E dico: "Dato li sia d'una lancia!"
Ciò a mi' padre, che mi tien sì magro
che tornare' senza logro di Francia.
Trarl'un denai' di man serìa più agro,
la man di pasqua che si dà la mancia,
che far pigliar la gru ad un bozzagro.

LXXXVII

There are three things that give me great delight,
And none of them come at a handy price:
Woman, the tavern and a game of dice;
And these alone can make my heart feel light.
But yet it seems I rarely have the right
To make good use of them, because my purse
Gives me the lie; the memory makes me curse
To think how money puts my joys to flight.
Therefore I say: "Go prod him with a lance!"
Meaning my father, who keeps me so lean
That I'd return without a lure from France.
The neediest suppliant could not obtain
Pennies at Easter from a man so mean:
You'll sooner see a buzzard kill a crane.

LXXXVIII

Qual è senza danari 'nnamorato
faccia le forch'e 'mpicchis'elli stesso,
ch'e' non muor una volta, ma più spesso
che non fa que' che del ciel fu cacciato.
E io, tapin! che, per lo mi' peccato,
s'egli è nel mondo Amor, cert'i' son esso,
non ho di che pagar potesse un messo,
se d'alcun uom mi fossi richiamato.
Dunque, per che riman ch'i' non mi'mpicco?
ché tragg'un mi' penser ch'è molto vano:
c'ho un mi' padre vecchissimo e ricco.
ch'aspetto ched e' muoi' a mano a mano –
ed e' morrà quando 'l mar sarà sicco,
sì l'ha Dio fatto, per mio strazio, sano.

LXXXVIII

A man who has no cash and falls in love
Should build a gallows for his own good use;
He dies but once, while loving he would lose
More lives than Satan hurled from heaven above.
It must be for my sins that I, no doubt,
Embody Love, if such a thing there be.
I couldn't pay the messenger his fee
To challenge one who put my word in doubt.
Then why not hang myself to finish it?
I'm stopped by one small thought that isn't healthy:
I have a father very old and wealthy
And like to think he's dying bit by bit;
But he won't die till all the sea is shore;
God made him tough to punish me the more.

LXXXIX

Sed i' credesse vìvar un dì solo
più di colui che mi fa vìvar tristo,
assa' di volte ringrazere' Cristo;
ma i' credo che fie pur com'i' volo,
ché potrebb'anzi di Genova 'l molo
cader ch'un becco vi desse di bisto:
chéd e' l'ha sì borrato 'l mal acquisto
che già non li entrare' freddo per polo.
Questi, di cu' dico, s'è 'l padre meo,
c'ha di noiarmi maggior allegrezza
che non ha l'occhio che 'n ciel vede Deo.
Vedete ben s'i' debbi'aver empiezza:
vedendolo l'altrier, mastro Taddeo
disse: "E' non morrà che di vecchiezza."

LXXXIX

If I felt sure to live a full day longer
Than that old rogue who keeps me sad and sighing,
My gratitude to Christ would now be stronger;
But I shall sooner learn the art of flying,
Or see the mole of Genoa* split asunder
By the assiduous butting of a goat:
He's plugged both ends so tight with all his plunder
No chill can enter by his arse or throat.
I mean my father, who finds more delight
In bullying me than spirits of the blessed
In seeing at last the face of God on high.
Now hear how yesterday confirmed my plight:
Doctor Taddeo saw him and confessed:
"Only old age can kill him, then he'll die."

XC

I' potre' anzi ritornare in ieri
e venir ne la grazia di Becchina,
o 'l diamante tritar come farina
o veder far misera vit'a frieri,
o far la pancia di messer Min Pieri,
o star content'ad un piè di gallina,
ched e' morisse ma' de la contina
que' ch'è domonio e chiamas'Angiolieri.
Però che Galïeno ed Ipocràto,
fossono vivi, ognun di lor saprebbe,
a rispetto di lu', men che 'l Donato.
Dunque quest'uom come morir potrebbe,
che sa cotanto ed è sì naturato
che, come struzzo, 'l ferr'ismaltirebbe?

XC

It's far more likely that I shall return
To yesterday and all Becchina's favours,
Pound diamonds into flour, or live to learn
That friars deny themselves the choicest flavours,
Or dine with relish on the claws of chicken,
Or grow a gut as big as Mino Pieri,*
Than that with mortal fever should be stricken
That devil from hell whose name is Angiolieri.
Even if Galen and Hippocrates*
Were still alive, the problem isn't humdrum,
And would be far too great for them to settle.
How can my father die? That's the conundrum:
So shrewd, so strong, so free from all disease
That like the ostrich he could feed on metal.

XCI

I' ho un padre sì complessionato
che, s'e' gollasse pur pezze bagnate,
sì l'avrebb'anz'ismaltit'e gittate
ch'un altro bella carne di castrato.
Ed i' era sì sciocch'e sì lavato
che s'i' 'l vedea mangiar pur du' derrate
di fichi, sì credea 'n veritate
il dì medesmo red'esser chiamato.
Tutto son fuori di quell'opinione,
e ho questa credenza fermamente:
ch'e' guf'ebber da lu' la complessione.
Vedete ben s'i'·debb'esser dolente!
Lasciamo star che non ha 'n sé ragione,
ma' che vedersi 'n cas'un fra godente!

XCI

My father's constitution is so blessed
That if he feasted on wet clothes for dinner,
Still his digestion would come out a winner
As quick as if he'd lunched on capon's breast.
I used to underestimate its merit
So stupidly that if he simply swallowed
Two bags of figs, I thought the day that followed
Would see him die at last and me inherit.
But time has cured this innocent belief,
Now I'm convinced the very owl that flits
Borrows from him the toughness we admire.
Then judge, my friends, what cause I have for grief!
Leaving aside the fact he's lost his wits,
Our family home contains a Joyful Friar.

XCII

Morte, merzé, se mi' prego t'è 'n grato,
che tu prend'un partito comunale;
e s'io non l'ho per ben, e non per male,
pur che tu prendi, facci divïato
ch'i' tante volte sia manganeggiato
quant'ha Grosseto granella di sale;
e 'l partito ch'i ti do sì è cotale,
o che t'uccidi me o lo 'ncoiato,
ch'i' non ne poss'andar altro che bene:
e se t'uccidi me, i' ne guadagno,
ch'elli è vit'e non mort', uscir di pene;
e se t'uccidi 'l ladro di Salvagno,*
or vedi, Morte, quel che me n'avvene:
ch'i' starò 'n Siena com'e' ricchi al Bagno.

XCII

Now Death, if it should please you, deign to take
For once, I beg, a quite impartial view;
Whether it brings me good or ill, just make
Your mind up either way, and quickly too,
Even if I'm bombarded with more stones,
Than are the grains a salt mine could provide:
The choice I offer you is this alone:
Either kill me or kill old Leatherhide;
I don't care which; my benefit is plain.
If am killed, it's surely to my profit,
Since it is life not death to flee from pain;
But if you choose to close that robber's day,
See, Death, how I shall take advantage of it
Here in Siena like the rich at play.

XCIII

Sed i' avesse mille lingue in bocca
e fosser tutte d'andànic'o acciaio,
e 'l predicar del buon frate Pagliaio,
non potre' fare sì ch'un fil di rocca
potesse aver da que' che viver locca
più che non fa l'osorrieri 'l danaio;
e quegli è 'l cavalier ch'è sanza vaio,
ciò è 'l gaudente cu' febbre non tocca!
Ché la Morte paur'ha di morire;
e s'ella intrasse in lui, i' son sicuro
ch'ella morrebb'e lu' farìa guarire;
ch'egli ha su' cuoio sì 'nferigno e duro
che chi per torre al ciel volesse gire
in lui fondar si converrebbe il muro.

XCIII

If I possessed a thousand tongues, and each
Were forged of hardest iron or of steel,
Or if, like Fra Pagliaio,* I could preach,
That feeble thread would fail in its appeal;
For lecher from his lust will be deterred
Sooner than usurer from the cash he clutches;
I mean this knight who never will be furred,
This Joyful Friar whom no fever touches.
For Death himself is fearful how he'd fare;
And if Death came to Dad, I'm pretty sure
Death would die first and Dad would find a cure;
His hide's so dry and hardened, I declare,
That if you planned to build the tower of Babel
You could find no foundation half so stable.

XCIV

Il pessimo e 'l crudele odio ch'i' porto
a diritta ragione al padre meo
il farà vìvar più che Botadeo –
e di ciò, buon dì, me ne sono accorto.
Odi, Natura, se tu ha' gran torto:
l'altrier li chiesi un fiasco di raspeo,
che n'ha ben cento cogna 'l can giudeo,
in verità, vicin m'ebbe che morto.
"S'i' gli avessi chèsto di vernaccia!"
diss'io, solamente a lui approvare:
sì mi volle sputar entro la faccia.
E poi m'è detto ch'i nol debbo odiare!
Ma chi sapesse ben ogni sua taccia
direbbe: "Vivo il dovresti mangiare!"

XCIV

The bitter hatred that I bear today
Toward my father, very rightly too,
Will cause him to survive the Wandering Jew,*
As I begin to learn to my dismay.
Nature, take note, see if you're just or not:
I asked him for a flask of common wine
(He's got a hundred barrels, the old swine!);
He very nearly killed me on the spot.
"I should have named Vernaccia smooth and mellow,"
Said I, to test how far his rage would go;
You won't believe the way he spat and swore.
And then I'm told I shouldn't hate the fellow!
But those who know one half of what I know
Would say: "The scoundrel should be eaten raw."

XCV

Non potrebb'esser, per quanto Dio fece,
che babbo spesso non mangi de l'oro,
ch'e' vive fresco e razza com'un toro,
e ha degli ottanta anni o 'n quella vece;
o ver ch'egli appiccat'ha con la pece
l'anima sua, che dice: "Dàll'agoro
ch'i' faccia fuor del su' corpo dimoro
a questi – di' che partir non mi lece!"
Però ch'i' credo ch'egli è maladetto,
e questo sì vi giuro sanza frodo,
ch'e' non credette mai di sopr'al tetto.
E la mia donna, secondo ch'i' odo,
in ora in ora sta sul trabocchetto:
or così vanno le cose al mi' modo.

XCV

In spite of God, there seems but little doubt
My father feeds on gold; indeed he's full
And fresh and paws the ground like any bull,
Although he's eighty now or thereabout.
His soul within his body, I've no doubt,
Is stuck with pitch: I hear it, how it cries:
"Allow me to depart, for, sir, time flies;
I should be gone, but still I can't get out!"
I think the scoundrel surely has been banned
From heaven; I swear his faith was never great
In that Old Gent who lives above the roof.
Meanwhile my wife, I'm given to understand,
Defrauds me hourly of my estate:
You see how well I'm doing; here's the proof.

XCVI

Non si disperin quelli de lo 'nferno,
po' che n'è uscito un che v'era chiavato –
el quale è Cecco, ch'è così chiamato,
che vi credea stare in sempiterno.
Ma in tale guisa è rivolto il quaderno
che sempre viverò glorificato,
po' che messer Angiolieri è scoiato,
che m'affliggea di state e di verno.
Muovi, nuovo sonetto, e vanne a Cecco,
a quel che giù dimora a la Badia –
digli che Fortarrigo è mezzo secco,
che non si dia nulla maninconia,
ma di tal cibo imbecchi lo suo becco,
ch'e' viverà più ch'Enoch ed Elia.

XCVI

Let not the devils and the damned despair,
For someone has escaped who lay in chains;
Cecco, I mean, a soul who shared their pains
And thought he'd have to stay for ever there.
The tide has turned, and turned in such a way
That I shall live in glory from now on;
The skinflint's skinned, Old Angiolieri's gone,
My bane through summer and winter, night and day.
Then rise, new sonnet, find that Cecco* out
Who lives down at the Abbey; tell him how
Old Fortarrigo's almost dry, and now
He need not be downcast, but have no doubt
That if he feeds on hope, as he should do,
He'll outlive Enoch and Elijah too.

XCVII

Chi dice del suo padre altro ch'onore
la lingua gli dovrebbe esser tagliata –
per che son sette le mortal peccata,
ma enfra l'altre quell'è lo maggiore.
S'eo fosse priete o ver frate minore,
al papa fora la mia prima andata,
e direi: "Padre Santo, una crociata
si faccia indosso a chi lor fa disnore."
E s'alcun fosse, per lo su' peccato,
che 'n quel stallo ci veniss'a le mani,
vorrei che fosse cotto e poi mangiato
dagli uomini no, ma da' lupi e cani.
Dio mel perdoni, ch'io n'ho già usato
motti non bei, ma rustichi e villani.

XCVII

A man who speaks no good about his sire
Surely deserves to have his tongue cut out;
The deadly sins are seven, but there's no doubt
That of them all this surely is most dire.
So if I were a priest or minor friar
I'd go straight to the Pope and there propose
A holy fierce Crusade against all those
Who drag their father's honour in the mire.
Indeed, if any guilty scoundrel then
Should fall into my hands, I would resolve
To have him cooked and eaten, not by men,
But by a pack of dogs or hungry wolves.
May God forgive me for my former use
Of terms not nice, of low and vile abuse.*

XCVIII

Tant'abbo di Becchina novellato
e di mie madr'e di babbo e d'Amore
ch'una parte del mondo n'ho stancato,
però mi vo' restare per migliore –
ché non è sì bel giuoco tropp'usato
che non sie rincrescente a l'uditore –
però vogli'altro dir, che più m'è 'n grato,
a ciascuno che porta gentil core.
E ne la poscia' muta del sonetto
i' vi dirò tutto ciò ch'i' vo' dire
e, chi lo 'ntende, sì sie benedetto:
ch'i' dico ch'i' arrabbio di morire
a veder ricco chi de' esser bretto,
vedendo bretto chi dovrìe gioire.

XCVIII

I've written so much of Becchina dear,
Of mother, father, and the god of Love,
I'm tiring half the readers that I have,
And it's much better I should stop right here,
For games that are amusing at the start
Go on too long and then become a bore;
And that is why I choose a theme that's more
Fitting for me and for the gentle heart.
The tercets of my sonnet will attest
Most fully everything I want to say,
And may the man who heeds my words be blessed:
It is that I could almost die with anger
To see those rich who ought to beg, while they
Who should be rich are left to rot with hunger.

XCIX

I' non vi miro perzar, morditori,
ch'i' mi conduca ma' nel vostro stato,
che 'l dì vi fate di mille colori
innanzi che 'l volaggio sia contato.
Ciò era vostra credenza, be' signori,
per ch'i' m'avesse a sollazzo giocato,
ch'i divenisse de' frati minori,
di non toccar dena' picciol né lato?
M'assa' ve ne potrà scoppiar lo cuore,
ch'i ho saputo sì dìciar e fare
ch'i' ho del mi' assa' dentro e di fore.
Ma 'l me' ch'i' ho, e che miglior mi pare,
sì è 'l veder di vo' che ciascun muore –
ché vi convien, per viver, procacciare.

XCIX

You scurrilous rogues, your shafts have gone astray,
Nor shall you drag me to your evil plight:
You who change colour twenty times a day
And reckon up your robberies by night.
When I played games of chance, I used to vow
That if I lost I'd not touch cash again;
So did you think I'd be a friar by now?
Sorry to disappoint you, gentlemen.
But you can go and eat your hearts out, sirs;
I've said and done so well that now I own
Plenty of land both in and outside town.
The best of all is that I see you curs
Dying with envy, fighting for a bone,
And living on the little you hunt down.

C

[*A Dante Alighieri*]

Lassar vo' lo trovare di Becchina,
Dante Alighieri, e dir del mariscalco:
ch'e' par fiorin d'òr, ed è di ricalco;
par zuccar caffettin, ed è salina;
par pan di grano, ed è di saggina;
par una torre, ed è un vil balco;
ed è un nibbio, e par un girfalco;
e pare un gallo, ed è una gallina.
Sonetto mïo, vàtene a Fiorenza,
dove vedrai le donne e le donzelle –
di' che 'l su' fatto è solo di parvenza.
Ed eo per me ne conterò novelle
al bon re Carlo conte di Provenza,
e per sto mo' gli fregiarò la pelle.

C

[*To Dante Alighieri*]

I sang Becchina: now I call a halt;
The Marshall,* Dante, is the theme I'll treat:
A golden florin? Why, he's counterfeit;
The priciest sugar? No, he's made of salt.
He's bread of humble millet, not of wheat;
A hut that seems a tower at first sight;
No falcon, but a very common kite;
A hen who seems a cock in his conceit.
Sonnet rise up; to Florence make your way,
And tell the dames and damsels that you see
That he's a total sham, and nothing more.
And I've got many things I mean to say
To good King Charles in Provence,* so that we
May rub that wretch's skin until he's sore.

CI

[*A Dante Alighieri*]

Dante Alighier, Cecco, 'l tu' serv'e amico,
si raccomand'a te com'a segnore;
e sì ti prego per lo dio d'Amore,
il qual è stat'un tu' signor antico,
che mi perdoni s'ispiacer ti dico,
ché mi dà sicurtà 'l tu' gentil cuore;
quel ch'i' ti dico è di questo tenore:
ch'al tu' sonetto in parte contraddico.
Ch'al meo parer ne l'una muta dice
che non intendi su' sottil parlare,
a que' che vide la tua Beatrice;
e puoi hai detto a le tue donne care
che tu lo 'ntendi: adunque, contraddice
a se medesmo questo tu' trovare.

CI

[To Dante on the Final Sonnet of the Vita Nuova]*

Dante, it's me, your servant and your friend,
Cecco, who now salutes you as his lord,
And prays you by the power you've long adored,
The God of Love, on whom you still attend,
That you'll excuse him if he should offend,
Since he relies upon your gentle heart.
For I must disagree, at least in part,
With what your sonnet says towards the end.
On coming to the tercets, you declare
You do not understand the subtle phrase
Of one that saw your Beatrice in her glory:
And then you say to all your ladies fair
That you have understood it, which conveys
A contradiction to your previous story.

CII

[*A Dante Alighieri*]

Dante Alighier, s'i' so bon begolardo,
tu mi tien' bene la lancia a le reni:
s'eo desno con altrui, e tu vi ceni;
s'eo mordo 'l grasso, tu ne sugi 'l lardo;
s'eo cimo 'l panno, e tu vi freghi 'l cardo;
s'eo so discorso, e tu poco raffreni;
s'eo gentileggio, e tu misser t'avveni;
s'eo so' fatto romano, e tu lombardo.
Sì che, laudato Deo, rimproverare
poco pò l'uno l'altro di noi due:
sventura o poco senno cel fa fare.
E se di questo vòi dicere piùe,
Dante Alighier, i' t'averò a stancare –
ch'eo so lo pungiglion, e tu se' 'l bue.

CII

[*To Dante*]*

Dante, if I'm a garrulous fool, I swear
You run a tilt against me quite as hard,
If I dine out with friends, you supper there,
And if I chew the fat, you suck the lard.
I shear the cloth, the nap is yours to raise;
And if I go too far, you're much too free;
If I have noble, you have learnèd ways;
If I'm for Rome, well, you're for Lombardy.
Then, thank the Lord, there's little to be said
By one against the other as things stand:
From want of wit or luck we take our knocks.
And if you've more to say upon this head,
Dante, I'll wear you down; just understand
That I'm the gadfly now and you're the ox.

CIII

Quando Ner Picciolin tornò di Francia,
era sì caldo de' molti fiorini
che li uomin li parean topolini,
e di ciascun si facea beff'e ciancia.
Ed usava di dir: "Mala mescianza
possa venir a tutt'i mie' vicini,
quand'e' son appo me sì picciolini
che mi fuora disnor la lor usanza!"
Or è per lo su' senn'a tal condotto
che non ha neun sì picciol vicino
che non si disdegnasse farli motto.
Ond'io mettere' 'l cuor per un fiorino
che, anzi che passati sien mesi otto,
s'egli avrà pur del pan, dirà: "Bonino!"

CIII

When Neri Picciolin returned from France,
Florins had blown him up to such a size
That in his presence other men seemed mice
That he would mock and look upon askance.
Often he said: "Now may some foul *malchance*
Come to my neighbours, strike them one and all,
Because, compared to me, they are so small
My honour's stained if I deign them a glance."
But see how far folly has brought him down:
For now the tiniest neighbour takes his turn
To jeer at him who used to be so bumptious.
Therefore I'll bet my heart against a crown
That, before eight months pass, if he can earn
A crust of bread, he'll eat it and say: "Scrumptious!"*

CIV

A cosa fatta non vale pentere,
né dicer po': "Così vorre' aver fatto."
Senno di dietro poco può valere:
però s'avveggia l'uomo 'nanzi tratto;
ché, quando l'uomo cominci a cadere,
e' non ritorna in istato di ratto:
io, che non seppi quella via tenere,
là dove non mi prude sì mi gratto.
Ch'i' son caduto e non posso levarmi,
e non ho al mondo parente sì stretto
che pur la man mi desse per atarmi.
Or non abbiate a beffa questo detto:
ché così piacci a la mia donna amarmi
come non fu giammai me' ver sonetto.

CIV

When something's done, it's idle to repent,
Or with "I should have" fruitlessly complain;
Hindsight helps nobody to change the event,
So look ahead lest you should fall again.
When once a man begins the long descent,
There won't be any sudden rise, that's plain;
So I, who never knew what wisdom meant,
Now scratch where nothing itches, all in vain.
I cannot rise, I've fallen far too low:
And as for someone stretching from above me
A helping hand, I wouldn't count upon it.
Therefore, I beg you, do not mock my woe,
When I declare I wish my wife could love me
With half the truth I've put into this sonnet.

CV

Egli è sì poco di fede e d'amore
oggi rimasa fra l'umana gente
che si potrebbe dir come nïente,
per quello che l'uom vede a tutte l'ore.
Chi peggio fa, tenuto ci è 'l migliore;
e non si truova amico né parente
che, l'un per l'altro, un danai'o 'l valsente
mettesse per vederlo imperadore.
Chi non mi crede, sì cerchi la prova:
vad'a qualunque gli è amico più caro
e poi mi dica che novelle e' trova:
se fia cortese diverralli avaro –
e ancor ci ha una foggia più nuova:
di se medesmo servir è l'uom caro.

CV

There is so little faith and love today
Within the human heart that, I'll be bound,
It's next to nothing if you start to weigh
The kind of thing you see when you look round.
He who behaves the worst is held the best,
And not a relative or friend is found
Who'd see another's plight, and then invest
A farthing to behold him emperor crowned.
If someone doubts me, let me recommend,
He go and see some soulmate tried and true
And, when he's finished, come back here to tell
How it worked out: he'll find his generous friend
Has turned a miser; and, what's really new,
He's just as stingy with himself as well.

CVI

Senno non val a cui fortuna è cónta,
né giova senno ad omo infortunato;
né gran savere ad omo non sormonta
s'a fortuna non piace e non è a grato.
Fortuna è quella che discende e monta
ed a cui dona ed a cui tolle stato;
fortuna onora e fa vergogna ed onta,
fa parer saggio un folle avventurato.
E spesse volte ho veduto venire
che usare senno è tenuto en follia
ed aver pregio per non senno usare.
Ciò ch'a fortuna è dato a provvedere,
non pò fallir, e mistier è che sia:
saggio il tegno chi sa temporeggiare.

CVI

Wisdom is needless if you're Fortune's friend,
And useless too if you are Fortune's foe;
Nor does great knowledge to advantage tend
If hostile Fortune has decided so.
Fortune's what lifts you up and brings you low,
And now she'll give, now snatch away the prize;
Both honour and disgrace she will bestow,
And make a lucky fool seem wondrous wise.
I've often heard discretion being decried
As mere insanity, and men praised who leave
Wisdom aside and everything to fate.
The gifts that Fortune's chosen to provide
Can't fail, whatever happens: I believe
The wisest man is one who learns to wait.

CVII

Stando lo baldovino dentro un prato,
de l'erba fresca molto pasce e 'nforna;
vedesi da la spera travallato
e crede che le orecchie siano corna;
e dice: "Questo fosso d'altro lato
salterò bene, ch'i' non farò storna."
Movesi per saltare lo fossato,
allor trabocca, e ne lo mezzo torna.
Allora mette un ragghio come tòno:
"Oimè lasso, che male pensato aggio,
ché veggio ben che pur asino sono!"
Così del matto avvien che si cre' saggio;
ma quando si prova nel parangono,
al dritto tocco pare il suo visaggio.

CVII

Once on a time upon a meadow fair
A donkey roamed and ate up all he found:
But when he saw his shadow on the ground
He took his ears for horns, so long they were.
"I truly am a stag, I do declare:
To prove the point, I'll go and jump that brook."
Without delay, a giant leap he took
And tumbled in the stream, half drowning there.
O then he brayed like thunder to the skies:
"Alas, how foolish was that first proud thought,
For now I see I'm nothing but an ass."
Thus is it with the fool who thinks he's wise;
For when he tests himself he's quickly caught,
And at the first attempt he sees his face.

CVIIIa

[Simone a Cecco]

Cecco, se Deo t'allegri di Becchina
o di quello che spesso sen rincoia,
consegliame, ché novamente ho poia,
e 'l cor cotant'ho trito com farina;
e se di corto non ho medicina,
temo che di tal male io non moia,
ca la persona ho tanto croia e boia
ch'a l'arca non vo senza la china,
ed a la piana non vo punto fuore
ch'ognun non dica: "Ve' un uom smarrito!" –
e quel che mi fa ciò sì è amore.
Dimmi, per Deo, tu che l'hai sentito
e, sì come tu di', lo senti ancore:
che difes'hai, che tu non èi pentito?

CVIIIa

[Simone of Siena* to Cecco]

Cecco, may God give you Becchina still
And take Old Leatherskin to his last rest;
Advise me now, for newly I'm distressed;
My heart is ground like flour in a mill.
And if I don't get medicine quite soon,
I fear I'll surely die of the disease;
My looks are stark and dark; I almost swoon
When a slight slope has sent me to my knees.
Even when it's a level path and plain,
Someone will shout: "That man has lost his way!"
And Love it is that's done all this to me.
Tell me, for God's sake, since you know the pain
And you still suffer from it, as you say:
You don't repent, so what's your remedy?

CVIIIb

[*Risposta di Cecco a Simone*]

Questo ti manda a dir Cecco, Simone,
da poi che vòi saper la sua difesa:
ogni grevezza per lo meglio ha presa,
ch'Amor gli ha dato per lunga stagione.
E' disse di sua bocca Salamone
questa parola, se l'hai bene 'ntesa:
né più né meno lo mal a l'om pesa
se non quanto esso al core se ne pone.
E parmi meglio, se mai torni en Siena,
che non ti lassi romper, ma piegare,
quand'addosso ti ven una gran pena.
Se vòi d'Amor o d'altro bene stare,
magistra sit tibi vita aliena,
disse Cato in su' versificare.

CVIIIb

[Cecco's Reply to Simone of Siena]

Since you have asked to know his remedy,
Simone, Cecco sends you this to say
He makes the best of what Love sends his way,
All those old troubles that he cannot flee.
With his own lips did Solomon impart
This message which I send to your address:
Ills weigh upon a man no more or less
Than as he takes his sufferings to heart.
And if you ever go back to Siena,
I think it's better you should bend, not break;
That's how to handle love and life; and when a
Great pain arrives, that is the way to take:
Magistra sit tibi vita aliena!*
Cato's advice repeated for your sake.

*Sonnets Ascribed to
Cecco Angiolieri*

CIX

Avvegna ched i' paghi 'l tu' mirare
più che s'ìo fossi del mondo signore,
che tu mi fai, amor? Per tuo onore
sì mi pur vuoi di te assicurare?
S'e' ti piace di volermi parlare,
io te ne prego da parte d'Amore;
e non guardar per ch'i' sia tuo minore,
ché quanto l'uomo è di maggior affare,
sì è tenuto d'aver, per ragione,
in sé umilitate e cortesia:
se ciò non fa, sì gli è gran riprensione.
Non per ch'io creda che 'n te villania
possa capere: in questa oppenïone
i' son tuo, e serò in dì di vita mia.

CIX

Since for one gracious glance from you, I'd pay
As if I were the lord of all the earth,
Does it not fit your honour and your worth
That you ensure my love as best you may?
If you should deign at last to speak to me,
I beg you do it only in Love's name;
Nor think my lowly state deserves your blame,
For where the man is greater in degree,
It's rightly thought his bearing should give proof
Of perfect humbleness and courtesy:
And he who fails in this deserves reproof.
Not that I think that there could ever be
Baseness in you: to this my mind holds fast,
That I am yours, now and while life shall last.

CX

Maladetto e distrutto sia da Dio
lo primo punto ch'io innamorai
di quella che dilettasi di guai
darmi, ed ogn'altro sollazzo ha in oblio;
e sì fa tanto tormento esser mio
che 'n corpo d'uom non ne fu tanto mai;
e non le pare aver fatto anco assai,
tant'è 'l su' cor giude', pessimo e rio.
E non pensa se non com'ella possa
far a me cosa che mi scoppi 'l cuore:
di questa oppinïon ma' non fu mossa.
E di lei non mi posso gittar fuore –
tant'ho la ment'abbarbagliat'e grossa
c'ho men sentor che non ha l'uom che muore.

CX

Now may God curse and utterly destroy
The moment when I fell in love, for she
Delights in pain that she inflicts on me,
And has no time for any other joy.
Indeed, when she torments me, the fierce smart
Is more than man has ever undergone;
Nor is she satisfied with what she's done,
So pitiless and evil is her heart.
The only thing she thinks about is how
To break my heart, her firm resolve is this,
And there is nothing else in that fair head.
Yet neither can I leap to freedom now;
My mind is so obscured by this distress
That I have no more feeling than the dead.

CXI

S'i' potesse d'amico in terzo amico
contare a la mia donna, con onore,
lo core meo stando servidore
a lei, in tal guisa che nemico
ne sono a lei: per me, ben tel dico,
se 'l savesse, credo avre' il su' amore;
e s'e' l'avesse, guardare' 'l su' onore
in ogni lato ch'è sotto al bellìco.
Omè lasso, che ho io fatto a lat'imo,
che in nulla guisa si porìa salvare,
sed io non le basciasse l'occhio e 'l viso?
Ch'Alena fo appo lei d'acqu'e limo;
bene le se farebbe pieno 'l Fare
de' rubini e smeraldi, ciò m'è viso.

CXI

If someone, say the friend of some good friend,
On my behalf, with honour, could recount
To my dear lady, how I long to count
Myself her servant; though she might contend
With me as with a foe, I think the end
Would be that when she knew, I'd have her heart;
And then her honour bright and every part
Below the belt I'd promise to defend.
Alas, what ails my lower part that lies
Hopeless below? The torment will grow keener
Unless I kiss her on the face and eyes.
Helen is mud compared to her, I swear;
And any man who came to her Messina
Would fill the narrow strait with pearls, that's clear.

CXII

A cui è 'n grado de l'Amor dir male,
or lo biasmi 'n buon'or, che Dio li dia;
ché io per me non terrò quella via,
ma in dirne ben non ci vo' metter sale.
Già non potrebbe conducerm'a tale
ch'in questa oppinïon sempre non stia,
per ch'egli è padre de la cortesia:
chi d'Amor sente, di mal far no i cale.
Anche ha cotale vertù l'Amore:
che in cui e' degna di voler errare,
fosse colui ch'anche fosse 'l piggiore,
di reio in buono in una 'l fa tornare –
e mai non pensa che d'avere onore,
e maggiormente il buon fa megliorare.

CXII

Now whosoever speaks in Love's dispraise,
I blame him roundly, may God curse his vice;
For my own part I will avoid such ways,
And sing Love's merits without thinking twice.
There's nobody and nothing that I know
Can ever make me budge from this opinion;
He's father of all courtesy below,
No evil thoughts belong in Love's dominion.
Love has, indeed, such sovereign power that when
He deigns to come and dwell within a soul,
Even the wickedest and worst of men
Will turn to good and cast off evil's fetter;
Honour is all he thinks of in this role;
And what is more, he makes a good man better.

CXIII

Quando mie donn'esce la man del letto
che non s'ha post'ancor del fattibello,
non ha nel mondo sì laido vasello
che, lungo lei, non paresse un diletto;
così ha 'l viso di bellezze netto
fin ch'ella non cerne col burattello
biacca, allume scagliuol'e bambagello,
par a veder un segno maladetto!
Ma rifassi d'un liscio smisurato,
che non è om che la veggia 'n chell'ora
ch'ella nol faccia di sé 'nnamorato.
E me ha ella così corredato
che di null'altra cosa metto cura
se non di lei: o ecc'om ben ammendato.

CXIII

Each morning when my lady leaves her bed,
Before she has applied the rouge with care,
There is no ugly body, be it said,
That by comparison will not seem fair.
Her face is without beauty, bleak and bare,
Until there's chalk and alum sifted out,
Creams, powders, lipstick, lotions splashed about;
You'd say a curse fell on her, then and there.
Yet once she's been dolled up and painted new
There's not a man who sees her but will fall
In love that instant and be never free.
Such is the state she has reduced me to
That now I care for nothing else at all
But only her; that's how she's settled me.

CXIV

I buon parenti, dica chi dir vuole,
a chi ne può aver, sono i fiorini:
quei son fratei carnali e ver cugini,
e padre e madre, figliuoli e figliuole.
Quei son parenti che nessun sen dole,
bei vestimenti, cavalli e ronzini:
per cui t'inchinan franceschi e latini,
baroni, cavalier, dottor di scuole.
Quei ti fanno star chiaro e pien d'ardire,
e venir fatti tutti i tuoi talenti
che si pon far nel mondo né seguire.
Però non dica l'uomo: "I' ho parenti" –
ché s'e' non ha denari, e' può ben dire:
"Io nacqui come fungo a' tuoni e venti!"

CXIV

Say what you will of relatives, the ones
That function best, once they are yours, are florins:
They are your real blood brothers and true cousins,
Father and mother too, daughters and sons.
These are the kin that we shall never rue,
Fine clothes, good ponies and a prancing steed;
They make the Latins and the French, indeed,
Knights, barons, and the learnèd, bow to you.
Money makes men serene and bold, and gives
The power to make our dreams and wishes come
True in a way that makes the whole world wonder.
Let no man say: "I've such fine relatives" –
Without the cash, he might as well proclaim:
"Look, I'm a mushroom, born of wind and thunder."

CXV

Con gran malinconia sempre istò,
sì ch'io allegrar nïente possomì;
o lasso! per che ciò m'avvien, non so:
potrestimen'atar, cotal? mi di'!
Deh fallo senza 'ndugio, se puoi mo,
ché 'l bisogno mostrar non possotì,
ché mille morti il dì, o vie più, fo;
però di confortarmi piacciatì,
sì ch'io non pera in tale stato qua:
ché uno tu' consiglio i' chero in fé,
ché là 'nd'i' venni possa reddir là.
Assa' di fare ciò prègone te:
ché 'l pensero sì forte giunto m'ha,
ch'altro non faccio, se non dire: "Omè!"

CXV

Here I am doomed to live in gloom and woe
Where never shines a ray of happiness;
And why it happens thus I do not know:
Ah, could you help me now in my distress?
But do it now, good friend, without delay
For there's more need of help than I can show
I die a thousand deaths or more each day;
Then comfort me; for if you do not so,
I fear that I shall perish in this state.
One counsel I would ask, with all my heart:
Show me the way and help me find the pass
To whence I came, for now my need is great.
I am so overburdened with this thought
That I can do no more than say "Alas!"

CXVI

L'uom non può sua ventura prolungare,
né far più brieve ch'ordinato sia;
ond'i' mi credo tener questa via:
di lasciar la natura lavorare
e di guardarmi, se io 'l potrò fare,
che non m'accolga più malinconia;
ch'i' posso dir che, per la mia follia,
i' ho perduto assai buon sollazzare.
Anche che troppo tardi me n'avveggio,
non lascerò ch'i' non prenda conforto,
ca far d'un danno due sarebbe peggio.
Ond'i' m'allegro e aspetto buon porto;
ta' cose nascer ciascun giorno veggio,
che 'n dì di vita mia non mi sconforto.

CXVI

No man can ever, by a single day,
Prolong his luck or shorten what's decreed;
Therefore the way of life I choose to lead
Is letting Nature work in her own way,
And when and where I can, refrain indeed
From any intercourse with melancholy,
For now I know that it was my own folly
That killed the joys on which I used to feed.
Though it's too late to remedy the past,
I will console myself as best I may;
It would be worse to make two ills of one.
So I rejoice, and hope to reach at last
Some pleasant port; it happens every day,
And I'm determined not to be undone.

CXVII

Un mercennaio intende a grandeggiare,
e pòggiavi sì smisuratamente
che sofferire già nol può la gente,
veggendol così forte vaneare.
Deh, fatel ritornare a vergheggiare
come solea fare anticamente,
ché, s'i' non sia del mi' capo dolente,
del su' fatto mi tien un gran cacare!
Or sentenziate s'a torto mi lagno
e se questo non è ben coral puzzo
ch'i' sofferisco da Lapo di Pagno:
chéd e' vezzeggia e tiensi gentiluzzo;
or ecco febbre da fuggirne al Bagno,
a quel che vi è colà 'n terra d'Abruzzo.

CXVII

A nobody sets out to pass for great
And swells up so excessively already
That nobody around can tolerate
Watching him ever grow more brash and heady.
O send him back to beating wool the way
He used to do before; for that he's fit;
May I be plagued with headache every day
If when I see him I don't want to shit.
Now say I'm wrong to tell men how I feel
And how I have to suffer from the stink
Lapo di Pagno* always spreads around,
Although he acts fastidious and genteel.
I'll flee this fever at the baths, I think,
Those of Abruzzo, if not further down.

CXVIII

Chi de l'altrui farina fa lasagne,
il su' castel non ha muro né fosso;
di senno, al mio parer, è vie più grosso
che se comprasse noci per castagne.
E' detti di colui son tele ragne
ch'offende e dice: "I' non sarò percosso" –
e' non ha denti e roder vuol un osso
e d'alti monti pensa far campagne.
Però di tal pensiere non sia lordo
omo che del valore ha 'l cuor diserto,
ché mal suo' arrivar volere 'ngordo.
Ma faccia come que' che sta coperto,
fin ch'altri ha rotto e franto suo bigordo:
poi mostri ben ch'e' sia di giostra esperto.

CXVIII

The man whose pasta's made with borrowed flour
Has built a castle without wall or ditch;
In my view, that's the kind of folly which
Seeks chestnuts, then buys walnuts and feels sour.
His words are weak as cobwebs, and in vain,
He first offends then says: "I'll not be beat" –
And has no teeth to gnaw the bone he'd eat,
And thinks to level mountains to the plain.
Let anyone who has a coward heart
Beware of vaunts like those of which I've spoken,
Which cannot reach the end he has in sight.
But let him stay well shielded at the start,
And when the adversary's lance is broken,
Then turn and show the world how well he fights.

CXIX

Ciò che naturalmente fu creato
in terra o 'n aere o 'n acqua che l'om vede
a segnoria de l'uom fu tutto dato
e si conduce e vive a sua mercede.
Ma lo mi' core è sì disnaturato
che nïente di ciò sente né crede,
ma di segnor è servo diventato,
e mai non de' cangiar voler né fede.
Ed è sì avvilato e dato a valle
che, senza far sembianti di dofesa,
si s'ha lasciato prendere a farfalle.
I' l'ho dal cor bensì per grande offesa,
da poi che 'n terr'ha sì date le spalle –
ma seguiroll'in quella via ch'ha presa.

CXIX

In Nature all things that have been created,
Earth, air and water, everything one sees,
To man's dominion were subordinated,
And work for his advancement and his ease.
But now my heart's disnature is so grave
It feels no danger and believes no ill;
But, once a lord, has now become a slave
And never thinks to change its faith or will;
So base and lowly has it come to lie
That, without any hint of a defence,
It has been captured like a butterfly.
Yet though my heart has been so badly shaken,
Forced to the ground and subject to offence,
I'll follow on the road that it has taken.

CXX

L'altrier sì mi ferìo una tal ticca
ch'andar mi fece a madonna di corsa:
andava e ritornava com'un'orsa
che va arrabbiando e 'n luogo non si ficca.
Quando mi vide, credett'esser ricca.
Disse: "Non avrestù cavelle in borsa?"
Rispuosi: "No." Quella mi disse: "Attorsa,
e lèvala pur tosto, o tu t'impicca!"
Mostravas'aspra come cuoio di riccio.
E' le feci una mostra di moneta –
quella mi disse: "Avesti caporiccio?"
Quasi beffava e stava mansueta
che l'avarì' tenuta un fil di liccio –
ma pur ne venni con la borsa queta.

CXX

The other day a certain itching will
Sent me off running to my lady fair,
Where I paced up and down the way a bear
Does when he's angry and just can't stay still.
She saw the jackpot when she found me there,
And asked: "Have you got something in your purse?"
I answered: "No". She said: "So much the worse;
Clear off and hang yourself for all I care!"
She was as prickly as a hedgehog's hide
Until I let her see a piece of money:
"Is there some hobby horse you'd like to ride?"
Said she, as mild as milk and sweet as honey.
I could have bound her with a silken thread:
My purse was empty when I left her bed.*

CXXI

I' son venuto di schiatta di struzzo
ne l'oste stando, per la fame grande:
ché d'un corsetto ho fatto mie vivande,
mangiandol tutto a magli'ed a ferruzzo.
E son sì fatto che non mi vien puzzo,
ma più abboccato che porco a le ghiande:
s'i' ho mangiat'i panni, il ver si spande,
ch'i' non ho più né mobile né gruzzo.
Ma egli m'è rimasa una gorgiera,
la quale m'ha a dar ber pur una volta,
e manderolla col farsetto a schiera.
La lancia non vi conto, ché m'è tolta,
ma 'l tavolaccio con la cervelliera
mi vanno in gola, e già dànno di volta.

CXXI

I have become an ostrich in my need,
For here in camp my hunger so increases
That on my corselet I've begun to feed;
I eat it link by link in little pieces.
No nausea can restrain my boundless greed;
Hogs dig for acorns, I'm a greater glutton:
My clothes must follow suit, and then indeed
The world will know I haven't got a button.
I've got a gorget that I mean to sell
So that I'll have enough to buy a drink;
Maybe I'll throw my doublet in as well;
My lance? No, that's already down the sink.
But helm and shield are sticking in my throat
And won't go down; I'll have to spew them out.*

CXXII

"Udite udite – dico a voi, signori –
e fate motto, voi che siete amanti:
avreste voi veduto, tra cotanti,
cotal c'ha 'l volto di tre be' colori?
Di ros'e bianch'e vermigli'è di fuori;
or lo mi dite, ch'i' vi son davanti,
sed elli inver di me fe' tai sembianti
ched i' potessi aver que' suo' colori."
"Noi non crediam che li potessi avere,
però ched e' non fece ta' sembianti,
che fosse ver' di te umilïato."
"Sed e' nol fece, i' mi pongo a giacere
e comincio a far ta' sospiri e pianti
che 'n quattro dì cred'esser sotterrato."

CXXII

"Come all you lords and lovers who embrace,
And listen, listen to the words I say:
Where have you ever seen a lad so gay,
With three such lovely colours in his face?
Rose, white and red, the perfect trinity;
Tell me, can they be mine, for here I stand;
Does not his bearing show that he has planned
To keep those colours all reserved for me?"
"No, no, we don't believe you'll have that joy,
For nothing in his bearing shows this boy
Will ever bend himself to suit your ways."
"If that be so, then here I choose to lie,
And now begin so sore to weep and sigh
That I'll be dead and buried in four days."*

CXXIII

I' so' non fermo in su questa oppenione
di non amar, a le sante guagnele,
uomo che sia inver di me crudele,
non abbiendo egli alcuna cagione;
ma questo dico, sanza riprensione:
di non servirti, né sarò fedele,
poi che di dolce mi vòi render fele –
fàilti tu, ma non ne hai ragione.
Da ch'i' conosco la tua sconoscenza
che tu ricredente contra me fai,
vogli'arrestare di te mai servire.
Per la qual cosa i' crederei 'nsanire,
se tu non n'avessi gran penitenza,
con essa avendo grandissimi guai.

CXXIII

I'm in two minds if I should love you still,
For, by the Gospels of Our Lord and Saviour,
I should not love a man who treats me ill,
And with no reason for his rank behaviour?
I won't go back on this, for I repeat
I will not be your servant or be true,
For bitter's the reward you give for sweet:
That's what you've done, and the fault lies with you.
Now that I know at last the full extent
Of your ingratitude, my way is plain:
My mind's made up, I will no longer serve.
Sometimes I think that I shall go insane
Unless some trouble brings you to repent,
With all the punishment that you deserve.

CXXIV

Un Corzo di Corzan m'ha sì trafitto
che non mi val cecèrbita pigliare,
né dolci medicine né amare,
né otrïaca che vegna d'Egitto.
E ciò che Galïen ci lasciò scritto
aggio provato per voler campare:
tutto m'è gocciola d'acqua nel mare,
tanto m'ha 'l su' velen nel mie cor fitto.
Là 'nd'i' son quasi al tutto disperato,
poi ched e' non mi val null'argomento –
a questo porto Amor m'ha arrivato.
Ché son quell'uom che più vivo sgomento
che si' nel mondo o che mai fosse nato –
chi me n'ha colpa di terra sia spento.

CXXIV

One Corso from Corsano's pierced me sore;
I've taken centaury to no avail,
All herbs and simples, sweet and bitter, fail,
And even theriac from Egypt's shore.
To stay alive I've studied Galen's lore,
But nothing that he wrote brings help to me;
His drugs are drops of water in the sea,
For I am poisoned to the very core.
Therefore I'm almost driven to despair,
Since I can find no remedy or cure;
Love brought me to this port and left me there.
I live in more distress and greater dread
Than any man alive, of that I'm sure:
Now may the guilty one be stricken dead!

CXXV

In tale che d'amor vi passi 'l core
abbattervi possiate voi, ser Corso,
e sì vi pregi vie men ch'un vil torso
e come tòsco li siate in amore.
E facciavi mugghiare a tutte l'ore
del giorno come mugghia bue od orso
e, come l'ebbro bee a sorso a sorso
il vin, vi facci ber foco e martore.
E se non fosse ch'i' non son lasciato,
sì mal direi, e vie più fieramente,
al vostro gaio compagno e avvenente
che di bellezze avanza ogni uom nato;
ma sì mi stringe l'amor infiammato
che verso lui ho sparto per la mente.

CXXV

May you, Ser Corso, meet with someone who
Subjects your heart to serve his every whim;
Like some old cabbage stalk may he treat you,
And may your love be poisonous to him.
And let him make you roar the hours away
Like any bull or bear that knows no shame,
And like the drunken sot who sips all day,
May you be drunk with drops of liquid flame.
And if I weren't constrained to some degree,
I'd add much more, with even greater scorn,
About your gay companion, fair and free,
Surpassed in looks by none of woman born;
But passion shall compel me to be kind:
An ardent love for him still floods my mind.

CXXVI

Deh guata, Ciampol, ben questa vecchiuzza
com'ell'è ben diversamente vizza,
e quel che par quand'un poco si rizza,
e come coralmente viene 'n puzza,
e com'a punto sembra una bertuzza
del viso e de le spalle e di fattezza,
e quando la miriam come s'adizza
e travolge e digrigna la boccuzza.
Ché non dovresti sì forte sentire
d'ira, d'angoscia, d'affanno o d'amore
che non dovessi molto rallegrarti
veggendo lei, che fa meravigliarti
sì che per poco non ti fa perire
gli spiriti amorosi ne lo core.

CXXVI

Come, Ciampol, look at this old hag and see
How withered up she is; and when she tries
To lift her herself on her two pins, how she
Gives off a stink that reaches to the skies.
Just like a monkey too in all her ways,
In every gesture; strange as it may be,
See how she gets excited as we gaze,
Twisting her hideous mouth at you and me.
Therefore, let not old sentiments of woe,
Of anger, anguish, or of love today
Prevent your laughing as you stand apart;
Just look at her who makes you marvel so,
And, before long, I think the sight will slay
The amorous spirits in your gentle heart.

CXXVII

"Pelle chiabelle di Dio, no ci arvai,
poi che feruto ci hai l'omo di Roma."
"I' son da Lucca. Che di'? che farai?"
"Porto cocosse a vender una soma."
"Doi te gaitivo, u' di' che 'nde vai?"
"Entro 'gn'Arezzo, a vender queste poma."
"Quest'àscina comprai da' barlettai
entro 'n Pistoia e féi tonder la chioma."
"De' che ti dea 'l malan, fi' de la putta,
ch'a Firenze n'ha' sèrique a danaio,
ed ancor più, e giugnet'u' mellone."
"A le guagnele! carich'è 'l somaio,
e porta a Siena a vender cheste frutta,
sì fuoron colte di buona stagione."

CXXVII*

"God's nails, you don't mess with a man from Rome
And get away with it; like bloody hell!"
"Lucca? Me too, mate. How are things back home?"
"And these 'ere pumpkins; I've a load to sell."
"Eh you, you twit, where d'ye think you're going?"
"Arezzo apples, ripe, give 'em a go!"
"This donkey's from Pistoia; I'm still owing.
A cooper's nag. Cost me a packet though."
"The devil take your mother for a whore,
In Florence half a sixpence buys you ten,
And with a nice big melon, if you please."
"I'll take my Bible oath, there ain't no more
This ass can carry! It's Siena then,
Where fruit as ripe as this don't grow on trees."

CXXVIII

Ogni capretta ritorn'a su' latte:
puot'ell'andare un pezzo ficullando?
Il padre i figli, e 'l figlio 'l padre batte,
e 'l frate 'l frate fièr sangue cavando;
nepot'e zio s'aman già come gatte,
marito moglie spesso va cacciando;
e 'ntra consorti ho viste guerre fatte,
e 'n tutte racconciare, 'n poco stando.
Però consiglio che 'ntra sì congiunti
di carn'e sangue null'uom si intrametta
s'egl'i vedesse di coltella punti;
ché 'l sangue è una cosa molto stretta:
e poi che d'ira si son sì consunti,
al latte suo ritorna ogni capretta.

CXXVIII

The kid returns to goat milk and its mother,
Although from time to time it goes astray;
A sire may beat his son, the son repay,
And brother draw the angry blood of brother;
Uncle and nephew quarrel with each other,
And husbands often chase their wives away:
And I've seen kinsmen locked in mortal fray,
Then quickly reconciled to one another.
So I advise you that it's always wrong
To get involved in others' family strife,
Even if someone brandishes a knife.
Indeed, the ties of blood are very strong,
And when the anger's all worked off, why then,
The kid returns to find its milk again.

CXXIX

Salute manda lo tu' Buon Martini,
Berto Rinier, de la putente Magna.
Sacci ch'i' ho cambiati i grechi fini
a la cervugia, fracida bevagna,
e le gran sale e' nobili giardini
a mosch'e a neve e a loto di montagna;
la buona usanza de li panni lini
ch'usar solea con voi è la campagna.
Ben puo' far beffe di mia vita fella,
ché spesse volte sièn senza tovaglia:
sette siem che mangiam per iscodella.
E non avem manti' per asciugaglia:
asciughiànci al gheron de la gonnella
quando no' siam ben unti di sevaglia.

CXXIX

Berto Rinier, your Buon Martini sends
You greeting from this stinking German land.
No more of Grecian wines; I now contend
With musty beer my guts can hardly stand.
From spacious halls and noble gardens I
Have come to flies and mud and snow and rain:
To linen sheets I've had to bid goodbye
And all our pleasant ways: we're on campaign.
You may well laugh, for now it's no great matter
That they don't lay a cloth upon the board;
We're seven eating from a single platter.
Napkins are something no one can afford;
And so with dirty chops we've made our peace,
We use our coat-tails to wipe off the grease.

Note on the Text

The Italian text of Angiolieri's sonnets is that of *Cecco Angiolieri: Rime*, edited by Gigi Cavalli (Milan: Biblioteca Universale Rizzoli, 1959). Notes and translation have also benefited from the commentaries in *Cecco Angiolieri: Le Rime*, edited by Antonio Lanza (Rome: Archivio Guido Izzi, 1990) and *Poeti giocosi del tempo di Dante*, edited by Mario Marti (Milan: Rizzoli, 1956). The English translation is based on the work of C.H. Scott, *The Sonnets of Cecco Angiolieri* (London: Chiswick Press, 1925) which has been extensively revised and modernized by Anthony Mortimer. Some sonnets remain much as Scott wrote them and others have been entirely retranslated; but the volume as a whole represents a collaboration between two translators, one living and one dead, whose talents, it is hoped, are not uncomplementary. For more information on C.H. Scott, please see the Biographical Note on page 301. Scott's translation includes the following title-page information and Preface:

THE SONNETS OF CECCO ANGIOLIERI
OF SIENA
DONE INTO ENGLISH DOGGEREL
BY
C.H.M.D. SCOTT

For the pompous rascallion
Who don't speak Italian
Nor French, must have scribbled by guess-work
BYRON

LONDON
PRINTED FOR PRIVATE CIRCULATION
AT THE CHISWICK PRESS
1925

Preface

Cecco Angiolieri of Siena is thought to have been born in 1258, and to have died in 1321. He was thus seven years older than Dante, 1265–1321, to whom he addressed at least three sonnets.

Though descended from a family of some eminence in Siena, but little is known of his life. According to his own confession, he at one time indulged a lively passion for a certain Becchina, the daughter of a complaisant Currier, *d'un agevol Coiaio*, together with an unusually bitter hatred of his parents. Whether either of these traits was as violent as the sonnets indicate may be open to doubt. Cecco was above all things a humorist, and this fact should never be forgotten when reading his poems.

Boccaccio relates a quaint story about him in the *Decameron* (4th novella, 9th day) in which the jest was certainly not to Cecco's advantage. It is worthy of note that Boccaccio calls him a fine and accomplished gentleman: "*il quale e bello e costumato uomo era*".

With regard to my own loose paraphrases, I have, save in a few instances, worked from the texts supplied by Professor Aldo F. Massèra in his *Sonetti di Cecco Angiolieri* (Bologna, Nicola Zanichelli, 1906), and his *Sonetti Burleschi e Realistici* (Bari, Giuseppe. Laterza e Figli, 1920). I have also followed the sequence of the latter work.

In *Dante and his Circle* Rossetti translated twenty-three sonnets of Cecco, of which sonnets twenty-one are printed by Professor Massèra.

Where I have occasionally ventured to differ from Rossetti's reading, it must not be thought that I desire to enter into any sort of competition. His masterly renderings are naturally far beyond the powers of a mere bungler like myself.

The curious reader (should I have one) who would know more of Cecco Angiolieri, his contemporaries, the ethics of his age and his position in Italian literature, is referred to Professor Massèra's copious notes, to Signor Alessandro D'Ancona's *Studj di Critica e Storia Letteraria* (Bologna, Nicola Zanichelli, 2nd edition, 1912), to Mr Langton Douglas's *History of Siena* (London, John Murray, 1902), to Mr William Heywood's *The Ensamples of Fra Filippo* (Siena, Enrico Torrini, 1901), and to Mr Edmund G. Gardner's *Story of Siena and San Gimignano* (London, J.M. Dent and Sons, 2nd edition, 1905).

I gladly take this opportunity of thanking Professor Massèra again for his courteous permission to print these version, which, all unworthy as they are, owe so much to his own labour and erudition.

To my friend, the late Mr William Heywood, I am especially indebted. He furnished me with prose translations of no less than thirteen sonnets. He also pointed out several errors into which my limited knowledge of Italian had blundered. For such faults as remain, and they must be many, I am solely responsible.

I am also under great obligation to Mr Edmund Gardner. On hearing casually that I (a total stranger to him) was uncertain as to the meaning of two sonnets, he most generously sent me prose translations of both of them. For this kindly act I am ever beholden to him.

C.S.
March 1924

265

Notes

p. 3, There are three speakers: first the poet and his friend and then Becchina, who enters at line 9 and whose "give me time to mourn this woe" is sadistically ironic. For other dialogues between Cecco and Becchina see pp. 45, 55, 65, 79, 95, 109.

p. 15, *Min di Pepo*: Possibly a reference to a Mino di Pepo d'Accorridore Petroni. C.H. Scott interpreted "Accorridore" as Mino's nickname.

p. 15, *Moco... Migo*: Most of the figures in this list have been identified. Cecco uses them to exemplify a series of vices: sodomy, gambling, cowardice and heresy.

p. 29, *Montaperti*: A reference to the famous battle of Montaperti (4th September 1260), won by the Ghibellines of Siena and Pisa over a Guelf army from Florence, Arezzo, Lucca and other Tuscan cities.

p. 39, The poem is a virtuoso exercise in the rhetorical device of *gradatio*, where the second major term in a line becomes the first major term in the line that follows (heart-hundred, hundred-death, death-rest, rest-night, night-torment, etc).

p. 43, *Skinner Benci's*: Becchina's father Benci was a tanner, a fairly lucrative profession in Tuscany, which is still noted for its fine leather-goods. The characters mentioned in lines 12–14 have not been identified, and the reference to Pisa is obscure.

p. 61, *Colle*: Colle di Valdelsa. Its inhabitants were long-standing enemies of Siena.

p. 67, *gentle heart*: The phrase echoes the first line of a poem by Guido Guinizelli that had became a manifesto for the poets of the *dolce stil novo*: "Love always comes to the gentle heart" (*Al cor gentil rempaira sempre amore*). The phrase recurs on pp. 197 and 203.

p. 71, *Holy Veil... Rome impart*: The Holy Veil with which Veronica wiped the face of Christ was the most venerated relic in Rome.

p. 73, *Friar Angiolieri*: Cecco's tyrannical father belonged to the order of the Knights of Saint Mary, also known as the Joyful Friars (*Frati Gaudenti*).

p. 79, Lines 7-8 are missing in the MS.

p. 81, *Arcidosso and Montegiovi*: Two famous fortified towns in Val d'Orcia.

p. 83, *Fucecchio… Boccheggiano*: Fucecchio is a town in Valdarno and could not be seen from Bologna, which is on the other side of the Apennines. Pogna (or Pugna) is a village near Siena and Boccheggiano is in the Maremma, not far from Grosseto.

p. 87, *Messina Straits*: The Straits of Messina have very dangerous currents.

p. 93, *I plucked a pear*: The plucking of the Pear has been interpreted as meaning that Cecco has been unfaithful to Becchina – possibly with a woman called Piera.

p. 105, *Ave, Dominus tecum*: The words of the Angel Gabriel to the Virgin Mary acquire a blasphemous tone in this context, where the *Dominus* is not God, but Cecco's rival for possession of the promiscuous Becchina. The Friar is, of course, Cecco's father.

p. 111, *becco*: Goats were traditionally associated with lust, and there is an obvious wordplay on *becco-Becchina*.

p. 131, *Vernaccia*: A famous Tuscan white wine.

p. 155, *spend as freely as a Florentine*: Florentines were considered tight-fisted by the Sienese.

p. 169, Cecco seems to have been exiled twice.

p. 171, *conjured up by Mahomet*: In medieval Europe Mahomet was considered a master of black magic.

p. 179, *mole of Genoa*: The mole of Genoa was renowned for its solidity. Doctor Taddeo may be the Florentine Taddeo d'Alderotto who died in 1295 and is mentioned in the *Divine Comedy* (Paradise, XII, 83).

p. 181, *Mino Pieri*: A prominent figure in Sienese politics.

p. 181, *Galen and Hippocrates*: The most famous physicians of ancient Greece.

p. 184, *Salvagno*: The thief of French chivalric novels.

p. 187, *Pagliaio*: A preaching friar from Siena.

p. 189, *the Wandering Jew*: According to the legend, Buttadeus (the Wandering Jew) was condemned to wander for all eternity as a punishment for having refused hospitality to Christ.

p. 193, *Cecco*: Probably a reference to Cecco di Fortarrigo, who appears in Boccaccio's *Decameron*, IX, 4, where he tricks Cecco Angiolieri. Boccaccio notes that both men hated their fathers.

p. 195, *vile abuse*: The monstrous hyperboles leave us in no doubt that this apparent recantation is, in fact, Cecco's last malicious joke at the expense of his hated father.

p. 201, *Marshall*: The conceited Marshall may well be Amerigo of Narbonne, a captain in the service of Charles II of Anjou, Count of Provence and King of Naples.

p. 201, *King Charles of Provence*: Possibly Charles II of Anjou (1254–1309), Count of Provence and King of Naples and Sicily (if the Marshall of line 2 is Amerigo).

p. 203, *the Final Sonnet of the Vita Nuova*: In the last sonnet of the *Vita Nuova* the "pilgrim spirit" (*peregrino spirito*) speaks words that the poet cannot understand, though he knows they refer to Beatrice. Cecco argues that this involves a contradiction, but his real target may be what he regards as the over-subtle philosophical distinctions in vogue among the poets of the *dolce stil novo*.

p. 205, *To Dante*: The answer to a lost poem by Dante. Line 8 links Cecco's exile in Rome to that of Dante in Verona.

p. 207, The sonnet mocks the snobbery of a Sienese merchant (Neri Picciolin) who has returned rich from France.

p. 217, *Simone of Siena*: The Simone who addresses Cecco has not been identified.

p. 219, *Magistra sit tibi vita aliena*: A quotation from the *Disticha Catonis* (III, 13, 2), a popular school book used for teaching Latin in the Middle Ages. The quotation can be rendered as "Change your way of life".

p. 227, The critic Gigi Cavalli claims that the poem is too obviously obscene to be the work of Cecco.

p. 239, *Lapo di Pagno*: Nothing is known of Lapo di Pagno.

p. 245, Now attributed to Cecco's Sienese contemporary Meo dei Tolomei.

p. 247, A disenchanted sonnet about military life (see also p. 263).

p. 249, The first of four sonnets dealing with a homosexual triangle composed of the poet, his rival Corso, and a beautiful youth.

p. 259, Now attributed to Lapo Gianni (1275–1328?), this lively market scene exploits elements from the dialects of Rome, Lucca, Arezzo, Pistoia, Florence and Siena.

Extra Material

on

Cecco Angiolieri's

Sonnets

Cecco Angiolieri's Life

The life of Cecco Angiolieri coincides with the period of *Cecco and Siena* Siena's greatest power, prosperity and cultural achievement. In what was probably the year of his birth (1260) the Sienese Ghibellines inflicted a memorable defeat on the Florentine Guelfs at the battle of Montaperti; and though Florence had regained the ascendant by the end of the decade, Siena, with its bankers and merchants and its republican form of government, continued to flourish for another eighty years. As a young man Cecco would have seen the great pulpit of Nicola and Giovanni Pisano in the cathedral, and he probably lived long enough to contemplate the *Maestà* of Duccio; about twenty years after his death the Lorenzetti brothers would paint the *Allegory of Good and Evil Government* in the Palazzo Pubblico. Sienese art demonstrates the combination of public piety and intense civic pride that is such an important part of the social context for the iconoclasm of Angiolieri's poetry.

The known facts about the life of Cecco Angiolieri are too few to furnish a biography. His mother Lisa de' Salimbeni belonged to the nobility that had been forced to share power with the merchant classes. His grandfather had been banker to Pope Gregory IX and his father Angioliero, also a banker, occupied a number of public positions in Siena and was a member of the exclusive religious confraternity popularly known as the Frati Gaudenti (Joyful Friars). Almost all the information we have about Cecco comes, predictably, from legal documents. In 1281 he is fined for leaving the camp during the Sienese siege of the fortress of Turri in Maremma. In 1282 there are three fines for wandering the streets after curfew. Five years later yet another fine punishes him for taking off during an expedition where the Sienese were helping Florence to defeat

Arezzo at Campaldino (Dante took part in the same campaign and the two poets may well have met: see Sonnets C, CI, CII). In 1291 he is involved in a brawl that ends with the wounding of a certain Dino di Bernardo di Monteluca, though he is not sent for trial. He seems to have been exiled twice (probably in 1292 and 1303–04) for reasons that remain obscure. After his father's death in 1296, he may well have fallen on hard times, for in 1302 he sells a vineyard and in 1312 (probably the year of his death) his children formally renounce an inheritance that was presumably burdened with debts.

Angiolieri and the Cecco legend — After circulating widely for more than a century (there are over thirty manuscript sources), the poetry of Cecco Angiolieri was largely forgotten. Crescimbeni (1696) may commend his wit and Francesco Trucchi (1846) note an innovative and energetic style, but in the major literary histories from Tiraboschi (1772–81) down to and including the great De Sanctis (1871) he is not even mentioned. It is an essay by Alessandro D'Ancona (1874) that revives interest in Angiolieri and at the same time creates what might be called the "Cecco Legend". D'Ancona reads the poetry as pure autobiography and deduces from it a vision of Cecco as a rebellious figure, isolated from the sophisticated literary culture of his day, reciting his poems before fellow derelicts in the taverns of Siena, a thirteenth-century *poète maudit* hiding an existential melancholy behind the comic mask. It is perhaps not surprising that such an interpretation should have appealed to a *fin de siècle* audience or that it should have arisen in an age that was so eager to find the "real story" behind Shakespeare's *Sonnets*, but its persistence has been remarkable. Without necessarily accepting the details of D'Ancona's reading, Pirandello and Croce share his biographical assumptions – as do, to a lesser degree, even post-war critics like Vitale and Lanza. More recently, the novelist Antonio Tabucchi, in his *Sogni di Sogni* (1992), perpetuates the legend with a fictional vision of Angiolieri that comes straight out of D'Ancona.

The first thing that needs to be said about the legend is that the extra-textual evidence for it is very flimsy. There was nothing extraordinary about young Sienese staying out after curfew or going absent while on military service, and a man may get himself into debt through sheer incompetence without any great effort at dissipation. The "handsome and courteous" Angiolieri who appears in Boccaccio's *Decameron* (IX, 4) has nothing in common with the Cecco of the legend, apart from the fact that he is reputed to hate his father. Members of Siena's notorious *brigata spendereccia* (Spendthrift Club) would, no doubt, have recognized something of their own lifestyle in the speaker of the sonnets, but that is no proof that Angiolieri himself should be numbered among them. The truth is that the real distinction of these sonnets lies not in some extraordinary self-revelation, but in a remarkable balance between self-conscious literariness and comic realism. The poetry of Angiolieri has some of its roots in the old medieval Latin Goliardic tradition still familiar to many readers through Helen Waddell's *The Wandering Scholars* (1926) or through the lyrics that Carl Orff set to music in *Carmina Burana*. The addiction to "woman, the tavern and a game of dice" (LXXXVII), the denunciation of poverty as the worst of ills and the frequent juxtaposition of religious imagery with decidedly secular sentiments – these were already the stock-in-trade of the Archpoet and his contemporaries more than a century before Angiolieri exploited them in the new vernacular. In his own time Angiolieri was certainly not the isolated literary rebel imagined by D'Ancona: his work needs to be seen in the context of a whole current of thirteenth-century poetry that Italian criticism labels as "comic", "realist" or "burlesque" and that counts Rustico Filippi among its most prominent exponents. Rustico, who precedes Angiolieri by some twenty years, is particularly interesting because his work divides into two equal parts, twenty-nine of his sonnets being perfectly serious love poems and twenty-nine burlesque. What this suggests is that the burlesque current is not so much a school that arises in opposition to the love poetry of the age, but rather one literary manner among others that a poet might choose to adopt. Even Dante experimented with the burlesque in his *tenzone* (poetic dispute) with Forese Donato.

Cecco Angiolieri's Sonnets

There is a risk of misreading Angiolieri if one concentrates on the more obviously colloquial sonnets such as the many dialogues with Becchina. The most salient characteristic of his poetry is the way it manoeuvres between colloquialism and gritty realism on the one hand and the high style (*stile aulico*) and theorizing of love poetry on the other. Fabian Alfie has

273

shown in convincing detail how Angiolieri foregrounds the literariness of his work by exploiting and undermining the themes and vocabulary of previous schools of Italian poetry from the Sicilians, who had invented the sonnet fifty years earlier, down to his contemporaries of the *dolce stil novo*. Here we can only cite a few examples. Sonnet XXV takes up the traditional theme of the lover who offers loyal service to his lady, and it does so with the whole panoply of traditional terms. But two asides in lines 8 and 10 (he is of a jealous nature and he does not feel at home in the role of a servant) reveal how seriously we are expected to take a metaphor that may have preserved some real power in feudal Provence or Sicily, but had precious little to do with the mercantile society of Siena. Sonnet XXX handles the same theme in a very different way. Here the metaphor of service is ridiculed first by being concretely embodied in the undignified (and unpleasant) image of the slaves on the quay at Pisa, and secondly by being put in the mouth of a cynical speaker who humiliates himself only on the understanding that one day he will be able to whistle – decidedly not a gesture one associates with courtly love.

The movement known as the *dolce stil novo* takes its name from a passage in the *Divine Comedy* (Purgatory XXIV, 49–60) where the poet Bonagiunta da Lucca praises a poem of Dante for its "new sweet style". What precisely was new about the movement is a matter of some controversy, since it inherits so much from the Provençal and Sicilian poetry of courtly love; but one may surely point to such aspects as the increasingly philosophical analysis of love from a Thomistic and Aristotelian standpoint, the influence of Franciscan mysticism, the sense of love as not merely ennobling but as the manifestation of a desire to be unified with the Highest Good, and the insistence on nobility as a matter of innate disposition rather than social rank. The poem traditionally taken as the manifesto of the *dolce stil novo* is *Al cor gentil rempaira sempre Amore* ('Love always comes to the gentle heart') by Guido Guinizelli (1240?–76), and it is with this *canzone* in mind that we should read Angiolieri's Sonnet XXXIII, which displays an almost perfectly Guinizellian lexical and thematic range – the gentle heart, the rejection of worldly honours, the emphasis on courtesy, the astrological reference, the prominent presence of God and the ineffable joy that comes from the lady's slightest gesture of approval. Stylistically there

274

is practically nothing to signal a satiric intention until the final tercet where the whole inflated construction is punctured by the wonderfully sly *se Dio mi fa sano* ("if the Lord keeps me fit") to reveal the essential physicality of the desire that has been so sublimated. Among other *dolce stil novo* poets, Guido Cavalcanti (1259–1300), the great friend of Dante's youth, receives particularly devastating treatment in Sonnet XIII, where the lover's fear and trembling in the presence of his lady are first given a straight-faced presentation and then comically visualized in a staggering figure who, one suspects, is likely to be mistaken for the local drunk. As for Dante, it is hard not to see Angiolieri's Becchina as the anti-type of Beatrice, not merely because of the alliteration, but because the names themselves have antithetical connotations: Beatrice is the one who blesses, who leads upwards to heaven; Becchina recalls *becco*, the goat, with its traditional associations of lust, and also *beccaio*, the medieval butcher.

The poetry of Angiolieri concentrates on two major themes – love (I–LXIV) and poverty (LXV–CV); but we have no proof that Angiolieri himself wished to construct a sequence where love poems and poverty poems would be placed in distinct sections. There is, in any case, a real thematic continuity, since love is so often evoked with monetary metaphors or evaluated in monetary terms. In sonnets XXIX and XXX, for example, the speaker imagines the enormous wealth for which he would *not* sell two hairs of Becchina's head and then wishes that she could buy him as a slave. It would be a truism to say that Angiolieri's obsession with money is the inevitable result of having grown up among bankers in a relatively highly developed mercantile society: in fact, the situation is rather more complex. Poverty becomes an issue not simply because Siena is prosperous, but because that prosperity coincides with the new and powerful discourse of evangelical poverty initiated by St Francis of Assisi (1182?–1226). In this context, Angiolieri's diatribes on poverty face two ways: on the one hand denouncing a society that seems to make economic success the only value, and on the other satirizing a discourse that idealizes deprivation.

What is truly striking in Angiolieri is the fact that his very limited subject matter should somehow accommodate such a rich and vibrant amount of social life. Far from being the solitary reflections of a meditative misfit, these poems seem to

275

take place against an unrelenting background of urban noise and bustle. Lovers quarrel in the streets, fathers and mothers can be overheard cursing their sons, a criminal is dragged past by a halter, a boy is caned by his teacher, a scullion turns the spit, a thirsty marble-cutter stops off for a drink, a doctor marvels at the longevity of his patient, a dishevelled soldier tries to sell his armour; usurers, gamblers, sodomites and heretics rub shoulders while Fra Pagliaio preaches. Angiolieri's importance in early Italian poetry can be measured by the fact that only Dante's *Inferno* will offer a more densely inhabited world.

Angiolieri in English   English interest in the Italian poets of the thirteenth century begins in the early nineteenth century, the period of the great political exiles such as Ugo Foscolo and Antonio Panizzi, of italophile scholars and anthologizers like Thomas James Mathias, William Roscoe and Capel Lofft, and of the first complete translation of the *Divine Comedy* by Henry Francis Cary (1814). It was, however, only in 1861 that Dante Gabriel Rossetti's groundbreaking *The Early Italian Poets* (1861) got round to including twenty-one sonnets by Angiolieri. Rossetti can be credited with giving unusually full recognition to Angiolieri thirteen years before D'Ancona's seminal essay, but he obviously found the "Scamp of Dante's Circle" hard to stomach. Many of the sonnets "are very repulsive from their display of powers perverted often to base uses", the sentiments expressed "are either impious or licentious", and Angiolieri must have outlived the composition of the *Inferno* because otherwise he would certainly have been "lodged in one of its meaner circles". Pre-Raphaelite taste, with its dreamy neo-medievalism, its aesthetic Christianity and its preference for the more languid emotions, was ill-prepared for the tough worldliness and verbal violence of Angiolieri. Under the circumstances, Rossetti does rather better than one might expect. He is, at least, a very professional sonneteer, and his translations are reassuringly firm in rhyme and metre. His version of the celebrated *S'i' fosse foco* ('If I were fire') is suitably vigorous, disfigured only by a blatant piece of rhyme-forcing in line 11. The fact remains that Rossetti is more at home with Dante and Cavalcanti, and it is not surprising that the sonnet he handles most effectively is *Qualunque ben si fa* ('Whatever good'), where both theme and diction are unusually close to the *dolce stil novo*.

The first complete English translation of Angiolieri is the work of C.H. Scott (see biographical note, p. 301). Published "for private circulation" in 1925, the little-known *Sonnets of Cecco Angiolieri of Siena, Done into English Doggerel* has virtues that belie its self-deprecating title-page. Not only is Scott often more literal than Rossetti, but he usually gets closer to Angiolieri's tone with a breezy Edwardian man-about-town manner, a sharp epigrammatic touch, and some highly ingenious rhyming reminiscent of Byron's *Don Juan*. It is indicative of Scott's balanced approach that he is hesitant about reading the sonnets as autobiography and insists that "Cecco was above all things a humorist". Some sonnets are marred by an almost automatic recourse to archaic elision ("whate'er", "o'er"), by a relapse into pseudo-medieval diction ("I ween", "in sooth", "veriest") or by line-filling periphrases; but the major defect is the constant wrenching of the syntax in order to facilitate rhyme.

At the end of his life, Thomas Caldecot Chubb (1899–1972), a prolific American poet and scion of a wealthy family of marine insurers, published a second complete version of Angiolieri, *The Sonnets of a Handsome and Well-Mannered Rogue* (1970). Relatively innocent of scholarship and determined to read the sonnets as straightforwardly autobiographical, Chubb shares most of Scott's vices but few of his compensatory virtues.

When Angiolieri's *l'angoscia mi fa sì sudare* becomes "agony with sweat my brow's besprent", it seems clear that Chubb is ineffective even in terms of his own outdated diction. Another American, Tracy Barrett, has the great merit of providing the first translation of Angiolieri into a recognizably modern idiom with *Cecco As I Am and Was: The Poems of Cecco Angiolieri* (1994). Barrett is always clear and sometimes elegant, but the choice of free verse as a medium has serious disadvantages. Without rhyme or metre, the sonnet form dissolves and one is left with, at best, a readable prose crib. And even on this level, Barrett leaves something to be desired since she relies almost exclusively on the often unsound glosses of Maurizio Vitale (1956). Thus a promising venture falls between two stools.

Among more recent versions of Angiolieri one notes two selections translated into a lively American idiom by Leonard Cottrell (2001) and Brett Foster (2005) and ten sonnets done into Scots by J.D. McClure (2007). These last especially succeed in combining blustering colloquial invective with strict observance of rhyme and metre in a way that recalls Robert Garioch's translations of the sonnets of Giuseppe Gioacchino Belli, where Scots offers such a splendid equivalent for Romanesco. But Angiolieri, for all his Sienese turns of phrase, is not a dialect poet, and though the Scots functions admirably for the particular poems that McClure chooses, it is hard to imagine how it might work for a larger selection that would need to reflect the shifting and complex relation between Angiolieri's use of colloquial diction and the high style of the traditions that he inherits and calls into question.

– Anthony Mortimer, 2008

Anthony Mortimer is Professor Emeritus at the University of Fribourg. His translations of Petrarch's *Canzoniere* and Michelangelo's *Rime* were published by Penguin to great critical acclaim. He has written extensively on Renaissance poetry and Anglo-Italian literary relations.

Select English Bibliography

Translations
Barrett, Tracy, *Cecco as I Am and Was, The Poems of Cecco Angiolieri* (Boston: International Pocket Library, 1994)
Chubb, Thomas Caldecot, *The Sonnets of a Handsome and Well-Mannered Rogue, Translated from Cecco Angiolieri of Siena* (Hamden, Conn.: Archon Books, 1970)
Cottrell, Leonard, 'Angiolieri, Eight Sonnets' (2001), http://brindin.com/piangtr1.htm
Foster, Brett, 'Cecco Angiolieri, *Rime*', *Yale Italian Poetry* 8 (2004–05), pp. 88-95
McClure, J.D., 'Angiolieri, Ten Sonnets' (2007), http://brindin.com.piangtr1.htm
Rossetti, Dante Gabriel, *The Early Italian Poets* (London: Smith, Elder, 1861)
Scott, C.H.M.D., *The Sonnets of Cecco Angiolieri of Siena, Done into English Doggerel* (London: Chiswick Press, 1925)
Stefanile, Felix, 'The Sonnets of Cecco Angiolieri', *PN Review* 15 (1989), v, pp. 14–20

Commentary

Alfie, Fabian, *Comedy and Culture: Cecco Angiolieri's Poetry and Late Medieval Society* (Leeds: Northern Universities Press, 2001)

Kleinhenz, Christopher, *The Early Italian Sonnet: The First Century, 1220–1321* (Lecce: Melilla, 1986)

Select Italian Bibliography

Angiolieri, Cecco, *Rime*, ed. Gigi Cavalli (Milan: Rizzoli, 1959)

Angiolieri, Cecco, *Le rime*, ed. Antonio Lanza (Rome: Archivio Guido Izzi, 1990)

Angiolieri, Cecco, *Rime*, ed. Raffaella Castagnola (Milan: Mursia, 1995)

Contini, Gianfranco, ed., *Poeti del Duecento*, 2 vols (Milan-Naples: Riccardo Ricciardi, 1960)

D'Ancona, Alessandro, 'Cecco Angiolieri da Siena, poeta umorista del secolo XIII', *Nuova Antologia* (1874), XXV, pp. 5–57.

Marti, Mario, *Cultura e stile nei poeti giocosi del tempo di Dante* (Pisa: Nistri-Lischi, 1953)

Marti, Mario, ed., *Poeti giocosi del tempo di Dante* (Milan: Rizzoli, 1956)

Marti, Mario, 'Cecco Angiolieri e la poesia comico-giocosa fra Due e Trecento', *Dizionario critico della letteratura italiana*, ed. Vittore Branca (Turin: UTET, 1973), Vol I, pp. 78–84.

Petrocchi, Giorgio, 'I poeti realisti', *Storia della letteratura italiana*, ed. Emilio Cecchi and Natalino Sapegno (Milan: Garzanti, 1965), Vol I, pp. 715–752

Pirandello, Luigi, 'Due saggi su Cecco Angiolieri', *Saggi, poesie, scritti vari*, ed. M. Lo Vecchio Musti (Milan: Mondadori, 1965), pp. 244–304

Quaglio, Enzo, ed., *La poesia realistica e la prosa del Duecento* (Bari: Laterza, 1971)

Vitale, Maurizio, *Rimatori comico-realistici del Due e Trecento* (Turin: UTET, 1956)

Appendices

Dante Gabriel Rossetti's Translations of Cecco Angiolieri
From *The Early Italian Poets from Ciullo d'Alcamo to Dante Alighieri* (London: Smith, Elder and Co. 1861)

Most literary circles have their prodigal – or what in modern phrase might be called their "scamp" – and among our Danteans this place is indisputably filled by Cecco Angiolieri of Siena. Nearly all his sonnets (and no other pieces by him have been preserved) relate either to an unnatural hatred of his father, or to an infatuated love for a certain married woman named Becchina. It would appear that Cecco was probably enamoured of her before her marriage as well as afterwards, and we may surmise that his rancour against his father may have been partly dependent, in the first instance, on the disagreements arising from such a connection. However, from an amusing and lifelike story in the *Decameron* (IX, 4) we learn that on one occasion Cecco's father paid him six months' allowance in advance in order that he might proceed to the Marca d'Ancona and join the suite of a Papal Legate who was his patron – which looks, after all, as if the father had some care of his graceless son. The story goes on to relate how Cecco (whom Boccaccio describes as a handsome and well-bred man) was induced to take with him as his servant a fellow-gamester with whom he had formed an intimacy purely on account of the hatred which each of the two bore his own father, though in other respects they had little in common. The result was that this fellow, during the journey, while Cecco was asleep at Buonconvento, took all his money and lost it at the gaming table, and afterwards managed by an adroit trick to get possession of his horse and clothes, leaving him nothing but his shirt. Cecco then, ashamed to return to Siena, made his way, in a borrowed suit and mounted on his servant's sorry hack, to Corsignano, where he had relations, and there he stayed till his father once more (surely much to his credit) made him a remittance of money. Boccaccio seems to say in conclusion that Cecco ultimately had his revenge on the thief.

In reading many both of Cecco's love sonnets and hate sonnets, it is impossible not to feel some pity for the indications they contain of self-sought poverty, unhappiness and natural bent to ruin. Altogether they have too much curious individuality to allow of their being omitted here: especially as they afford the earliest prominent example of a naturalism without afterthought in the whole of Italian poetry. Their humour is sometimes strong, if not well chosen; their passion always forcible from its evident reality: nor indeed are several among them devoid of a certain delicacy. This quality is also to be discerned in other pieces which I have not included as having less personal interest; but it must be confessed that for the most part the sentiments expressed in Cecco's poetry are either impious or licentious. Most of the sonnets of his which are in print are here given[1] – the selections concluding with an extraordinary one in which he proposes a sort of murderous crusade against all those who hate their fathers. This I have placed last (exclusive of the 'Sonnet to Dante in Exile') in order to give the writer the benefit of the possibility that it was written last, and really expressed a still rather bloodthirsty contrition – belonging at best, I fear, to the content of self-indulgence when he came to enjoy his father's inheritance. But most likely it is to be received as the expression of impudence alone, unless perhaps of hypocrisy.

Cecco Angiolieri seems to have had poetical intercourse with Dante early as well as later in life; but even from the little that remains, we may gather that Dante soon put an end to any intimacy which may have existed between them. That Cecco already poetized at the time to which the *Vita Nuova* relates, is evident from a date given in one of his sonnets – the 20th June 1291 – and from his sonnet raising objections to the one at the close of Dante's autobiography. When the latter was written he was probably on good terms with the young Alighieri; but within no great while afterwards they had discovered that they could not agree, as is shown by a sonnet in which Cecco can find no words bad enough for Dante, who has remonstrated with him about Becchina.[2] Much later, as we may judge, he again addresses Dante in an insulting

---

1. It may be mentioned (as proving how much of the poetry of this period still remains in MS.) that Ubaldini, in his Glossary to Barberino, published in 1640, cites as grammatical examples no fewer than twenty-three short fragments from Cecco Angiolieri, one of which alone is to be found among the sonnets which I have seen, and which I believe are the only ones in print. Ubaldini quotes them from the Strozzi MSS (DGR).

2. Of this sonnet I have seen two printed versions, in both of which the text is so corrupt as to make them very contradictory in important points; but I believe that by comparing the two I have given its meaning correctly (DGR)

tone, apparently while the latter was living in exile at the court of Can Grande della Scala. No other reason can well be assigned for saying that he had "turned Lombard", while some of the insolent allusions seem also to point to the time when Dante learnt by experience "how bitter is another's bread and how steep the stairs of his house".

Why Cecco in this sonnet should describe himself as having become a Roman is more puzzling. Boccaccio certainly speaks of his luckless journey to join a Papal legate, but does not tell us whether fresh clothes and the wisdom of experience served him in the end to become so far identified with the Church of Rome. However, from the sonnet on his father's death he appears (though the allusion is desperately obscure) to have been then living at an abbey; and also, from the one mentioned above, we may infer that he himself, as well as Dante, was forced to sit at the tables of others: coincidences which almost seem to afford a glimpse of the phenomenal fact that the bosom of the Church was indeed for a time the refuge of this shorn lamb. If so, we may further conjecture that the wonderful crusade-sonnet was an *amende honorable* then imposed on him, accompanied probably with more fleshly penance.

Though nothing indicates the time of Cecco Angiolieri's death, I will venture to surmise that he outlived the writing and revision of Dante's *Inferno*, if only by the token that he is not found lodged in one of its meaner circles. It is easy to feel sure that no sympathy can ever have existed for long between Dante and a man like Cecco; however arrogantly the latter, in his verses, might attempt to establish a likeness and even an equality.

[Dante Gabriel Rossetti's translations of Cecco's poems, at times based on a variant and possibly corrupt Italian text, correspond to the following sonnets in our edition: CI, LXII, XXXVIII, XXXVII, XXVIII, XL, XXXIV, XIX, VIII, C, LXXXV, XCIV, LXXXVI, CIV, LXXXVIII, LXXII, XCII, LIII, XCVI, XCVII, CII. We have omitted two of his translations, which were based on sonnets incorrectly attributed to Cecco Angiolieri.]

I

Dante Alighieri, Cecco, your good friend
And servant, gives you greeting as his lord,
And prays you for the sake of Love's accord
(Love being the master before whom you bend)
That you will pardon him if he offend,
Even as your gentle heart can well afford.
All that he wants to say is just one word,
Which partly chides your sonnet at the end.
For where the measure changes, first you say
You do not understand the gentle speech
A spirit made touching your Beatrice:
And next you tell your ladies how, straightway,
You understand it. Wherefore (look you) each
Of these your words the other's sense denies.

II

I am enamoured, and yet not so much
But that I'd do without it easily;
And my own mind thinks all the more of me
That Love has not quite penned me in his hutch.
Enough if for his sake I dance and touch
The lute, and serve his servants cheerfully:
An overdose is worse than none would be:
Love is no lord of mine, I'm proud to vouch.
So let no woman who is born conceive
That I'll be her liege slave, as I see some,
Be she as fair and dainty as she will.
Too much of love makes idiots, I believe:
I like not any fashion that turns glum
The heart, and makes the visage sick and ill.

III

The man who feels not, more or less, somewhat
Of love in all the years his life goes round
Should be denied a grave in holy ground,
Except with usurers who will bate no groat:
Nor he himself should count himself a jot
Less wretched than the meanest beggar found.
Also the man who in Love's robe is gown'd
May say that Fortune smiles upon his lot.
Seeing how love has such nobility
That if it entered in the lord of hell
'Twould rule him more than his fire's ancient sting;
He should be glorified to eternity,
And all his life be always glad and well
As is a wanton woman in the spring.

IV

Whatever good is naturally done
Is born of Love as fruit is born of flower:
By Love all good is brought to its full power:
Yea, Love does more than this – for he finds none
So coarse but from his touch some grace is won,
And the poor wretch is altered in an hour.
So let it be decreed that Death devour
The beast who says that Love's a thing to shun.
A man's just worth the good that he can hold,
And where no love is found, no good is there;
On that there's nothing that I would not stake.
So now, my sonnet, go as you are told
To lovers and their sweethearts everywhere,
And say I made you for Becchina's sake.

V

Why, if Becchina's heart were diamond,
And all the other parts of her were steel,
As cold to love as snows when they congeal
In lands to which the sun may not get round;
And if her father were a giant crown'd
And not a donkey born to stitching shoes,
Or I were but an ass myself – to use
Such harshness, scarce could to her praise redound.
Yet if she'd only for a minute hear
And I could speak if only pretty well,
I'd let her know that I'm her happiness –
That I'm her life should also be made clear,
With other things that I've no need to tell;
And then I feel quite sure she'd answer "Yes".

VI

If I'd a sack of florins, and all new
(Packed tight together, freshly coined and fine)
And Arcidosso and Montegiovi mine,[3]
And quite a glut of eagle-pieces too –
It were but as three farthings to my view
Without Becchina. Why then all these plots
To whip me, daddy? Nay, but tell me – what's
My sin, or all the sin of Turks, to you?
For I protest (or may I be struck dead!)
My love's so firmly planted in its place,
Whipping nor hanging now could change the grain.
And if you want my reason on this head,
It is that whoso looks her in the face,
Though he were old, gets back his youth again.

---

3. Perhaps the names of his father's estates (DGR) [See note to page 81].

VII

I'm full of everything I do not want
And have not that wherein I should find ease;
For alway till Becchina brings me peace
The heavy heart I bear must toil and pant;
That so all written paper would prove scant
(Though in its space the Bible you might squeeze)
To say how like the flames of furnaces
I burn, remembering what she used to grant.
Because the stars are fewer in heaven's span
Than all those kisses wherewith I kept tune
All in an instant (I who now have none!)
Upon her mouth (I and no other man!)
So sweetly on the twentieth day of June
In the new year[4] twelve hundred ninety-one.

VIII

My heart's so heavy with a hundred things
That I feel dead a hundred times a day;
Yet death would be the least of sufferings,
For life's all suffering save what's slept away;
Though even in sleep there is no dream but brings
From dreamland such dull torture as it may.
And yet one moment would pluck out these stings,
If for one moment she were mine today
Who gives my heart the anguish that it has.
Each thought that seeks my heart for its abode
Becomes a wan and sorrow-stricken guest:
Sorrow has brought me to so sad a pass
That men look sad to meet me on the road –
Nor any road is mine that leads to rest.

---

4. [...] There is some added vividness in remembering that Cecco's un-platonic love encounter dates eleven days after the first death anniversary of Beatrice (9th of June 1291), when Dante tells us that he "drew the resemblance of an angel upon certain tablets" (DGR).

IX

When I behold Becchina in a rage,
Just like a little lad I trembling stand
Whose master tells him to hold out his hand;
Had I a lion's heart, the sight would wage
Such war against it that in that sad stage
I'd wish my birth might never have been plann'd,
And curse the day and hour that I was bann'd
With such a plague for my life's heritage.
Yet even if I should sell me to the Fiend,
I must so manage matters in some way
That for her rage I may not care a fig;
Or else from death I cannot long be screen'd.
So I'll not blink the fact, but plainly say
It's time I got my valour to grow big.

X

Dante Alighieri in Becchina's praise
Won't have me sing, and bears him like my lord.
He's but a pinchbeck florin, on my word;
Sugar he seems, but salt's in all his ways;
He looks like wheaten bread, who's bread of maize;
He's but a sty, though like a tower in height;
A falcon, till you find that he's a kite;
Call him a cock! – a hen's more like his case.
Go now to Florence, sonnet of my own,
And there with dames and maids hold pretty parles
And say that all he is doth only seem.
And I meanwhile will make him better known
Unto the Count of Provence, good King Charles;[5]
And in this way we'll singe his skin for him.

5. This may be either Charles II, King of Naples and Count of Provence, or
more probably his son Charles Martel, King of Hungary. We know from
Dante that a friendship subsisted between himself and the latter prince,
who visited Florence in 1295, and died in the same year, in his father's
lifetime (Paradise, VIII, 49 ff.) (DGR) [see notes to page 201].

XI

I'm caught, like any thrush the nets surprise,
By Daddy and Becchina, Mammy and Love.
As to the first-named, let thus much suffice –
Each day he damns me, and each hour thereof;
Becchina wants so much of all that's nice,
Not Mahomet himself could yield enough:
And Love still sets me doting in a trice
On trulls who'd seem the Ghetto's proper stuff.
My mother don't do much because she can't,
But I may count it just as good as done,
Knowing the way and not the will's her want.
Today I tried a kiss with her – just one –
To see if I could make her sulks avaunt:
She said, "The devil rip you up, my son!"

XII

The dreadful and the desperate hate I bear
My father (to my praise, not to my shame)
Will make him live more than Methusalem;
Of this I've long ago been made aware.
Now tell me, Nature, if my hate's not fair.
A glass of some thin wine not worth a name
One day I begged (he has whole butts o' the same)
And he had almost killed me, I declare.
"Good Lord, if I had asked for vernage wine!"
Said I – for if he'd spit into my face
I wished to see for reasons of my own.
Now say that I mayn't hate this plague of mine!
Why, if you knew what I know of his ways,
You'd tell me that I ought to knock him down.[6]

---

6. I have thought it necessary to soften one or two expressions in this sonnet
(DGR).

XIII

If I were fire, I'd burn the world away;
If I were wind, I'd turn my storms thereon;
If I were water, I'd soon let it drown;
If I were God, I'd sink it from the day;
If I were Pope, I'd never feel quite gay
Until there was no peace beneath the sun;
If I were Emperor, what would I have done? –
I'd lop men's heads all round in my own way.
If I were Death, I'd look my father up;
If I were life, I'd run away from him;
And treat my mother to like calls and runs.
If I were Cecco (and that's all my hope),
I'd pick the nicest girls to suit my whim,
And other folk should get the ugly ones.

XIV

For a thing done, repentance is no good,
Nor to say after, "Thus would I have done" –
In life, what's left behind is vainly rued;
So let a man get used his hurt to shun;
For on his legs he hardly may be stood
Again, if once his fall be well begun.
But to show wisdom's what I never could;
So where I itch I scratch now, and all's one.
I'm down, and cannot rise in any way;
For not a creature of my nearest kin
Would hold me out a hand that I could reach.
I pray you do not mock at what I say;
For so my love's good grace may I not win
If ever sonnet held so true a speech!

XV

Whoever without money is in love
Had better build a gallows and go hang;
He dies not once, but oftener feels the pang
Than he who was cast down from heaven above.
And certes, for my sins, it's plain enough,
If Love's alive on earth, that he's myself,
Who would not be so cursed with want of pelf
If others paid my proper dues thereof.
Then why am I not hanged by my own hands?
I answer: for this empty narrow chink
Of hope – that I've a father old and rich,
And that if once he dies I'll get his lands;
And die he must, when the sea's dry, I think.
Meanwhile God keeps him whole and me i' the ditch.

XVI

I am so out of love through poverty
That if I see my mistress in the street
I hardly can be certain whom I meet,
And of her name do scarce remember me.
Also my courage it has made to be
So cold that, if I suffered some foul cheat,
Even from the meanest wretch that one could beat,
Save for the sin I think he should go free.
Ay, and it plays me a still nastier trick;
For, meeting some who erewhile with me took
Delight, I seem to them a roaring fire.
So here's a truth whereat I need not stick –
That if one could turn scullion to a cook,
It were a thing to which one might aspire.

XVII

Gramercy, Death, as you've my love to win,
Just be impartial in your next assault;
And that you may not find yourself in fault,
Whate'er you do, be quick now and begin.
As oft may I be pounded flat and thin
As in Grosseto there are grains of salt,
If now to kill us both you be not call'd –
Both me and him who sticks so in his skin.
Or better still, look here; for if I'm slain
Alone – his wealth, it's true, I'll never have,
Yet death is life to one who lives in pain:
But if you only kill Saldagno's knave,
I'm left in Siena (don't you see your gain?)
Like a rich man who's made a galley-slave.[7]

XVIII

I would like better in the grace to be
Of the dear mistress whom I bear in mind
(As once I was) than I should like to find
A stream that washed up gold continually:
Because no language could report of me
The joys that round my heart would then be twin'd,
Who now, without her love, do seem resign'd
To death that bends my life to its decree.
And one thing makes the matter still more sad:
For all the while I know the fault's my own,
That on her husband I take no revenge –
Who's worse to her than is to me my dad.
God send grief has not pulled my courage down,
That hearing this I laugh; for it seems strange.

---

7. He means, possibly, that he should be more than ever tormented by his
creditors, on account of their knowing his ability to pay them; but the
meaning seems very uncertain (DGR).

XIX

Let not the inhabitants of hell despair,
For one's got out who seemed to be locked in;
And Cecco's the poor devil that I mean,
Who thought for ever and ever to be there.
But the leaf's turned at last, and I declare
That now my state of glory doth begin:
For Messer Angiolieri's slipped his skin,
Who plagued me, summer and winter, many a year.
Make haste to Cecco, sonnet, with a will,
To him who no more at the Abbey dwells;
Tell him that Brother Henry's half dried up.[8]
He'll never more be down-at-mouth, but fill
His beak at his own beck,[9] till his life swells
To more than Enoch's or Elijah's scope.

XX

Who utters of his father aught but praise,
'Twere well to cut his tongue out of his mouth;
Because the Deadly Sins are seven, yet doth
No one provoke such ire as this must raise.
Were I a priest, or monk in any ways,
Unto the Pope my first respects were paid,
Saying, "Holy Father, let a just crusade
Scourge each man who his sire's good name gainsays."
And if by chance a handful of such rogues
At any time should come into our clutch,
I'd have them cooked and eaten then and there,
If not by men, at least by wolves and dogs.

---

8. It would almost seem as if Cecco, in his poverty, had at last taken refuge in a religious house under the name of Brother Henry (Frate Arrigo), and as if he here meant that Brother Henry was now decayed, so to speak, through the resuscitation of Cecco (DGR) [see note to page 193].

9. In the original words, "*Ma di tal cibo imbecchi lo suo becco*", a play upon the name of Becchina seems intended, which I have conveyed as well as I could (DGR).

The Lord forgive me! for I fear me much
Some words of mine were rather foul than fair.

XXIII

Dante Alighieri, if I jest and lie,
You in such lists might run a tilt with me:
I get my dinner, you your supper, free;
And if I bite the fat, you suck the fry;
I shear the cloth and you the teazle ply;
If I've a strut, who's prouder than you are?
If I'm foul-mouthed, you're not particular;
And you're turned Lombard, even if Roman I.
So that, 'fore Heaven! if either of us flings
Much dirt at the other, he must be a fool:
For lack of luck and wit we do these things.
Yet if you want more lessons at my school,
Just say so, and you'll find the next touch stings –
For, Dante, I'm the goad and you're the bull.

From Boccaccio's Decameron (IX, 4)

Cecco Fortarrigo gambles away at Buonconvento all his own posses-
sions and also money belonging to Cecco Angiolieri; stripped to his
shirt he runs after Angiolieri, saying that he has been robbed by him,
causes him to be seized by some peasants, dresses himself in his clothes,
mounts his palfrey and makes off, leaving the other wearing only his
shirt.

Neifile, at the queen's command, began her story… "In Siena, not
many years ago, there were two men who were both mature as far as
their years went, and both called Cecco, one being the son of Messer
Angiolieri and the other of Messer Fortarrigo. Although they were very
different in many ways, in one respect they were alike: they both hated
their fathers. For this reason they had become friends and were often
seen together. Now when it struck Angiolieri, who was a handsome
and courteous man, that he led a poor life in Siena on the allowance his
father made him, and he heard that a cardinal who was a great patron
of his was in the Marches of Ancona as the Pope's legate, he decided to
travel there to improve his circumstances. His father, when he was told
of this, agreed to let him have an advance of six months' allowance, so
that he might provide himself with appropriate clothing and a horse
and cut a respectable figure.

While he was looking for someone he could take with him as his
servant, Fortarrigo came to hear of it, and he went to Angiolieri and
begged him, as fervently as he could, to take him with him, saying
that he would be his attendant and body servant and do whatever was
required, with no payment but his expenses. Angiolieri replied that he
did not want to take him, not because he did not consider him capable,
but because he sometimes gambled and got drunk; however, to this
Fortarrigo replied that he would certainly avoid both those vices; he
embellished what he said with plenty of oaths, and his pleas eventually
got the better of Angiolieri, who said he was happy for him to come.

One morning they set out together and came to Buonconvento,
where they dined; after the meal, since it was very hot, Angiolieri had
a bed prepared for him in the inn, undressed with Fortarrigo's help,
and went off to sleep after saying he wished to be called at the hour of
nones. While Angiolieri slept, Fortarrigo went to the tavern, and there,

after a few drinks, he started to gamble; in a very short time he had lost what little money he had on him, and also all the clothes he was wearing. Then, hoping to recoup his losses, he went in his shirt to where Angiolieri was and, finding him fast asleep, he took all the money out of his purse, and went back and gambled all that away too.

When Angiolieri awakened, he dressed and asked for Fortarrigo; failing to find him, he presumed that he was lying dead drunk somewhere, as he was in the habit of doing; he therefore decided to abandon him and get another servant at Corsignano. He had his palfrey saddled and his luggage packed, but when he went to pay his reckoning he could not find any money. This resulted in a great outcry, and the whole inn was in an uproar, with Angiolieri saying that he had been robbed while staying there, and threatening to have everyone arrested and taken to Siena. Then along came Fortarrigo in his shirt, keen to take Angiolieri's clothes as he had taken his money. When he saw Angiolieri about to mount, he said: 'What's all this, Angiolieri? Have we got to go already? Please wait a moment: someone will be here in a minute to whom I've pawned my doublet for thirty-eight shillings, and I'm sure he'll give it back for thirty-five on the nail.'

While he was speaking, someone arrived who made Angiolieri certain that it was Fortarrigo who had stolen his money: he told him how much Fortarrigo had lost. Angiolieri was enraged at this, and fired reproaches at Fortarrigo, and would have slaughtered him if he had not feared man's law more than he feared God; as it was, he mounted his horse, threatening to have him hanged or banished from Siena under pain of death.

Fortarrigo, acting as though Angiolieri had said this to someone else and not to himself, said: 'Now, now, Angiolieri, let's just stop talking like that: it doesn't get us anywhere. Look at it this way: we'll have the doublet back for thirty-five shillings if we pay now; but if we delay even till tomorrow, he'll not take less than the thirty-eight shillings he gave me for it; he's doing me a favour here, because it was on his advice I bet it. Come, come, why shouldn't we grab the opportunity to gain three shillings?'

When he heard him speak like this, Angiolieri was at a loss – particularly since he saw all the bystanders staring at him, and it was clear that they did not believe that Fortarrigo had gambled away Angiolieri's money, but that Angiolieri still had some money of his

– and he said to him: 'What's your doublet got to do with me? You should be strung up: you've not only robbed me and gambled away what was mine, but on top of that you're preventing me from leaving, and you're making a fool of me.'

Fortarrigo still stood his ground, just as though those words were not meant for him, and he said: 'Why, oh why don't you want me to be three shillings better off? Don't you think I shall be able to oblige you with them another time? Do it, if you have any regard for me at all! What's all the rush? We can still get to Torrenieri in good time this evening. Come on, find that purse of yours. You know I could search throughout Siena and not come up with a doublet to suit me as well as this one. And to think I let it go to that fellow for thirty-eight shillings! It's worth forty or more, so you're harming me in two ways.'

Angiolieri, nettled to find himself not only robbed by this fellow but detained in a pointless conversation, gave no reply, but turned his palfrey's head and made for Torrenieri. At this, Fortarrigo, with a cunning plan in mind, started to trot behind him, in his shirt. When they had gone a good two miles, with Fortarrigo still begging for his doublet, and Angiolieri quickening his horse's pace in order to spare himself that annoyance, Fortarrigo saw some peasants working in a field by the side of the road some way in front of Angiolieri. Fortarrigo shouted out to them: 'Stop him, stop him!' So they ran into the road with their spades and mattocks, under the impression that Angiolieri had robbed the man who was running after him in his shirt, and they blocked his way; and he did not get anywhere by telling them who he was and the true facts of the situation.

Fortarrigo ran up with a frown on his face and shouted: 'I don't know how I keep myself from killing you, you treacherous thief, running away with what is mine!' Then, turning to the peasants, he said: 'You see, gentlemen, in what a state he left me at my inn, after gambling away everything of his own! It's only through God and you that I've got this much back, for which I shall always be grateful.'

Angiolieri gave his account of things, but no one listened to him. Fortarrigo, with the help of the peasants, dragged him off his horse, took his clothes off him and dressed himself in them. Mounting the horse, he left Angiolieri standing in his shirt and with bare feet, and returned to Siena, telling everyone that he had won the palfrey and the clothes from Angiolieri in a game of chance. Angiolieri, who had thought to join the cardinal in the Marches as a rich man, went back to Buonconvento a poor man in his shirt; there, not daring for the time being to return to Siena for very shame, he borrowed some clothes and, on the nag which Fortarrigo had ridden, he travelled to relatives of his in Corsignano, and stayed with them until his father provided some more money. And so Fortarrigo's cunning triumphed over Angiolieri's sensible plan, although when the time and place were right he was not left unpunished."

Translated by J.G. Nichols, 2008

Biographical Note on C.H. Scott

Born in London on 16th June 1862, Charles Henry Montagu Douglas Scott was the second son of Lord Walter Scott by his wife Anna, 4th daughter of Sir William Hartopp Bart. of Freeby, Leicestershire, and grandson of the 5th Duke of Buccleuch and Queensberry. In his third year he fell victim to infantile paralysis, which left him physically handicapped for the rest of his life. As it was impossible for him to be sent to school, he was able to cultivate his natural love of literature and art unimpeded by the conventional education routine of the period, and though he missed the advantages of a classical training, he became a man of wide reading and culture and of marked individual character.

In spite of his physical disabilities – he was never able to walk without crutches – as a young man he travelled widely on the continent, visiting all the chief picture galleries of Europe. He became a keen student of modern languages and was proficient in French, German and Italian. Poetry always attracted him and verse flowed from his own pen before he was sixteen. He was deeply interested in history, architecture and the applied arts. It was not uncommon for men of his generation and upbringing to spend their lives in houses full of beautiful things of which they hardly realized their existence. Not so Charles Scott. The treasures among which he grew up at Boughton were a constant source of delight to him. In his family he was regarded as a living encyclopedia, and it was seldom that he could not answer any question relating to family history, pictures, manuscripts, old furniture, tapestry or armour. His annotated manuscript catalogue of the pictures at Boughton, with photographic illustrations by his brother Francis Scott, is a monument of research.

Charles Scott spent his early life at Boughton – "the old place I love to the verge of idolatry" – as he expressed himself in a letter to a friend. His affection for his home was extended to the shire which forms its setting. In fact, though predominantly Scottish by descent, and deeply versed in the lore of the border country, nearly all his life was spent in Northamptonshire, for after his father's death he moved to Geddington. As age increased, so did his infirmities, and during the last few years he became much of a recluse, though he continued his annual visits to one or two special friends almost up to the end.

Those who had the privilege of Charles Scott's friendship affectionately remembered his gaiety and humour, his most entertaining conversation, his modesty about his own abilities, and the singular beauty of his voice, all of which were combined in a personality of quite extraordinary charm. He died peacefully at Geddington Priory after a short illness on 4th March, 1936, and was buried in Weekley churchyard, near so many of the long line of his ancestors, the Montagus of Boughton. He has left behind him the example of a life lived with a high and unfailing courage, and the memory of a rare and truly gallant spirit.

[Adapted from the Preface to C.H. Scott's *Tales of Northamptonshire*, Northamptonshire Printing & Publishing Co.: Kettering, 1936]

Acknowledgements

Many old friends and some new ones have helped me with this book. Fabian Alfie's recent study of Angiolieri offered essential information and stimulating insight. Edoardo Fumagalli, as ever, provided learning to answer my queries and wisdom to soothe my anxieties. Roger Meyenberg gave me the benefit of his specialised knowledge of sonnet translation in the nineteenth century. Thomas P. Roche and John Logan supplied material unavailable outside the United States. Tracy Barrett and Brett Foster sent me copies of their own Angiolieri translations. The staff of the Bibliothèque de Genève and its associated libraries have been unfailingly courteous and obliging. It will be no surprise to those who know him that the idea for this book came from Alessandro Gallenzi at Oneworld Classics. He it was who saw the merit of Scott's almost completely forgotten translation of Angiolieri, invited me to edit it, and then encouraged me to revise or rewrite as I saw fit. At every stage, he has been prodigal with advice and encouragement, and I can only hope that the book as it now stands is not too unworthy of the energy he has invested in it. Finally, let me acknowledge my co-translator C.H. Scott. Italian poetry has brought us together across a gap of eighty years: I have enjoyed working with him.

Anthony Mortimer, 2008

The publisher wishes to acknowledge Anthony Mortimer for his excellent revision of C.H. Scott's translations. Many thanks also to J.G. Nichols, Julian Molina and William Chamberlain for their patient editorial work, and their help in the preparation of this volume.

ONEWORLD CLASSICS

ONEWORLD CLASSICS aims to publish mainstream and lesser-known European classics in an innovative and striking way, while employing the highest editorial and production standards. By way of a unique approach the range offers much more, both visually and textually, than readers have come to expect from contemporary classics publishing.

∽

CHARLOTTE BRONTË: *Jane Eyre*

EMILY BRONTË: *Wuthering Heights*

ANTON CHEKHOV: *Sakhalin Island*
Translated by Brian Reeve

CHARLES DICKENS: *Great Expectations*

D.H. LAWRENCE: *The First Women in Love*

D.H. LAWRENCE: *The Second Lady Chatterley's Lover*

D.H. LAWRENCE: *Selected Letters*

JAMES HANLEY: *Boy*

JACK KEROUAC: *Beat Generation*

JANE AUSTEN: *Emma*

JANE AUSTEN: *Pride and Prejudice*

JANE AUSTEN: *Sense and Sensibility*

WILKIE COLLINS: *The Moonstone*

GIUSEPPE GIOACCHINO BELLI: *Sonnets*
Translated by Mike Stocks

DANIEL DEFOE: *Robinson Crusoe*

ROBERT LOUIS STEVENSON: *Treasure Island*

MIKHAIL BULGAKOV: *Master and Margarita*
Translated by Hugh Aplin

GIACOMO LEOPARDI: *Canti*
Translated by J.G. Nichols

OSCAR WILDE: *The Picture of Dorian Gray*

GEOFFREY CHAUCER: *Canterbury Tales*
Adapted into modern English by Chris Lauer

HENRY MILLER: *Quiet Days in Clichy*

NATHANIEL HAWTHORNE: *The Scarlet Letter*

MARY WOLLSTONECRAFT SHELLEY: *Frankenstein*

FRANZ KAFKA: *Letter to My Father*
Translated by Hannah Stokes

BRAM STOKER: *Dracula*

GIOVANNI BOCCACCIO: *Decameron*
Translated by J.G. Nichols

DANTE ALIGHIERI: *Rime*
Translated by Anthony Mortimer and J.G. Nichols

IVAN BUNIN: *Dark Avenues*
Translated by Hugh Aplin

FYODOR DOSTOEVSKY: *The Humiliated and Insulted*
Translated by Ignat Avsey

FYODOR DOSTOEVSKY: *Winter Impressions*
Translated by Kyril Zinovieff

ÉMILE ZOLA: *Ladies' Delight*
Translated by April Fitzlyon

BOILEAU: *The Art of Poetry* and *Lutrin*
Translated by William Soames and John Ozell

ANONYMOUS: *The Song of Igor's Campaign*
Translated by Brian Reeve

ANN RADCLIFFE: *The Italian*

LEO TOLSTOY: *Anna Karenina*
Translated by Kyril Zinovieff

STENDHAL: *The Life of Rossini*
Translated by Richard N. Coe

CONNOISSEUR

THE CONNOISSEUR list will bring together unjustly neglected works, making them available again to the English-reading public. All titles are printed on high-quality, wood-free paper and bound in black cloth with gold foil-blocking, end papers, head and tail bands and ribbons. Each title will make a perfect gift for the discerning bibliophile and will combine to make a wonderful and enduring collection.

～

AMBROSE BIERCE: *The Monk and the Hangman's Daughter*

SAMUEL GARTH: *The Dispensary*

JOHN ARBUTHNOT: *The History of John Bull*

TOBIAS SMOLLETT: *The History and Adventures of an Atom*

ALESSANDRO TASSONI: *The Rape of the Bucket*
Translated by James Atkinson and John Ozell

UGO FOSCOLO: *Poems*
Translated by J.G. Nichols

JOHANN WOLFGANG GOETHE: *Urfaust*
Translated by J.G. Nichols

GIUSEPPE PARINI: *A Fashionable Day*
Translated by Herbert Bower

GIAMBATTISTA VICO: *Autobiography*
Translated by Stephen Parkin

GIFT CLASSICS

HENRY MILLER: *The World of Sex*

JONATHAN SWIFT: *The Benefit of Farting*

ANONYMOUS: *Dirty Limericks*

NAPOLEON BONAPARTE: *Aphorisms*

ROBERT GRAVES: *The Future of Swearing*

CHARLES DICKENS: *The Life of Our Lord*

CALDER PUBLICATIONS

SINCE 1949, JOHN CALDER has published eighteen Nobel Prize winners and around fifteen hundred books. He has put into print many of the major French and European writers, almost single-handedly introducing modern literature into the English language. His commitment to literary excellence has influenced two generations of authors, readers, booksellers and publishers. We are delighted to keep John Calder's legacy alive and hope to honour his achievements by continuing his tradition of excellence into a new century.

∾

ANTONIN ARTAUD: *The Theatre and Its Double*

LOUIS-FERDINAND CÉLINE: *Journey to the End of the Night*

MARGUERITE DURAS: *The Sailor from Gibraltar*

ERICH FRIED: *100 Poems without a Country*

EUGÈNE IONESCO: *Plays*

LUIGI PIRANDELLO: *Collected Plays*

RAYMOND QUENEAU: *Exercises in Style*

ALAIN ROBBE-GRILLET: *In the Labyrinth*

ALEXANDER TROCCHI: *Cain's Book*

To order any of our titles and for up-to-date information about our current and forthcoming publications, please visit our website on:

www.oneworldclassics.com